INTRODUCTION TO POETRY

By Mark Van Doren

INTRODUCTION TO POETRY

Commentaries on Thirty Poems

BY

MARK VAN DOREN

 HILL AND WANG · NEW YORK

Copyright Acknowledgments

PREFACE

This is a book about short poems. Epics and dramas have no place in it, nor for that matter will the reader find anywhere in it a systematic discussion of poetry in the form with which we are concerned: the short, the lyric form which for many persons today represents the only kind of poetry there is. I have not sought to define poetry, lyric or otherwise, nor have I labored to defend it. General statements about the art can be very valuable, but they run two risks: of being unintelligible to those without experience, and of seeming extravagant and untrue to those without either experience or desire.

The desire for poetry and lifelong love of it come only with experience of its best specimens. As one who has never been in love knows nothing about love, and learns nothing about it from statements and definitions, so one who has never read a good poem well and felt its power for himself will continue to care nothing for poetry in spite of every attempt to make him do so. The remedy in the first case is the experience of falling in love with a person; in the second, with a poem. The aim of this volume is to introduce its readers to some poems with which they may fall in love.

Toward that end a set of commentaries on thirty poems has been provided. The number of poems could have been less or greater, just as the commentaries could have been shorter or longer than they are. They are not exhaustive—the reader, the student, the teacher may have more and better things to say than I have said—but it is my hope at any rate that they will be sufficient introductions to the poems. I state my own views as fully and emphatically as I can, but not with the intention of forcing agreement with them. My hope is rather that the reader will come to know what *he* thinks and feels as he goes through the poems and the commentaries with me. I have said nothing but what I thought was plainly true. He should do likewise. The main thing is that he should open his mind, his eyes, and his ears to what is going on in the poem under discussion. The poem, I think, can then be trusted to achieve its right effect.

I have paid as little attention as possible to certain matters which by some are thought to assist interpretation but which often only confuse it. I mean such matters as the life of the poet, the time when he wrote, and the supposed reason for his writing this particular poem. We know less about such things than we sometimes pretend; and anyway I have assumed of each poem I discuss that it should go under its own power. If it is not intelligible without the aid of biography and history, to that extent it is limited in its natural effect. I have considered the natural effect, and done all I could to say what it is for myself. My choice of poems to be analyzed I do not defend except by saying that it comes out of a long experience as reader and teacher. These are the poems I have had most to say about; and these are the poems which have made it easiest for me to suggest after all what I think poetry is. For I have said in many places what I think it is; but always with specific lines, stanzas, and poems in view. The reader if he likes can collect those scattered generalizations and form them into a theory. I have not done so at any point, preferring still to avoid suspicion of nonsense and exaggeration.

I believe I have always been specific—have pointed to things that were visible and listened to things that were audible. I have never knowingly ignored rhythm and sound. These are things that suffer by the silence of the printed page, but in the circumstances there is no help for that. I should like to think that the test of reading aloud will be applied in every case. A line of poetry is not properly alive until it is heard and its movement felt. So for a passage, and so for a poem. The reading of poetry is still a social experience, as any successful college class will prove, or as friends know who have passed evenings introducing to one another their favorite verses.

A glossary of technical terms, chiefly metrical, has been added in the interest of simplifying the commentaries. Most of the terms are used many times, but always with the same meaning; so that if the glossary is consulted whenever doubt occurs, we may proceed swiftly with our common experience of the poems elected for attention—and, it may be, love.

M.V.D.

1968

CONTENTS

INTRODUCTION TO POETRY

1. A Song

Ask me no more where Jove bestows,
When June is past, the fading rose;
For in your beauty's orient deep
These flowers, as in their causes, sleep.

Ask me no more whither do stray   5
The golden atoms of the day;
For, in pure love, heaven did prepare
Those powders to enrich your hair.

Ask me no more whither doth haste
The nightingale, when May is past;   10
For in your sweet dividing throat
She winters, and keeps warm her note.

Ask me no more where those stars light
That downwards fall in dead of night;
For in your eyes they sit, and there   15
Fixèd become, as in their sphere.

Ask me no more if east or west
The Phoenix builds her spicy nest;
For unto you at last she flies,
And in your fragrant bosom dies.   20
                        —THOMAS CAREW

In the five stanzas of this formal song a lover pays five compliments to his lady. She is not named; nor does the song itself
have any name except this noncommittal one which begins,
casually enough, with the indefinite article. "A Song"—as if
any lover, anywhere or at any time, might be understood to
have seized a musical instrument of some sort and, looking into
his lady's eyes, strummed it five times as he sang five answers
to five questions which she or someone else has asked. It is not
necessarily she who has put the questions. Perhaps she is per-

fectly silent, smiling as she listens; or she may not be here at all; she may indeed not exist, though we should prefer to think she does. The questions may well be the lover's own, which he has invented for the sake of their answers. They are rhetorical; they assist statement.

The five statements to which they lead are all, if one pleases, extravagant. Where does Jove, the king of the universe, send roses when they fade? Into your beauty, where they sleep. What is the destination, if any, of the sunlight's particles? Your hair, which they were created to adorn. Where does the nightingale fly when she stops singing? Into your throat, where she continues to sing until another season returns. Where do falling stars go? Into your eyes, as into the place for which they were intended. Where does the phoenix, that fabulous Arabian bird which lives forever by alternately burning itself and rising newborn from the ashes, build its nest upon which this act of immortality may be accomplished? In your bosom, of course.

Doubtless it is the extravagance of the compliments at which the lady smiles. Yet she is pleased, for she knows that her lover is trying to be absolute in the expression of his love. The things he says are true for him because he loves her without qualification. If to an indifferent person they would sound exaggerated or fantastic, he trusts her not to find them so; he counts on her to understand, as of course he understands, that overstatement is adoration's natural language. Only too much love is love enough; or rather, only too strong a statement is strong at all. The exact truth about her, supposing it could be put into words, would be inadequate to his purpose, which is to suggest that this after all is the exact truth—for him, anyway. He too smiles as he sings, watching his lady's eyes for signs that she measures the playful force with which he overstates his case. Absolute eloquence is the minimum effect at which he aims. All or nothing, as with any lover in the world, is the motto of his words and music.

But whereas he is like any other lover in his feeling he is different in his art. He is formal to what might seem a fault if we did not become aware of the resources he is using. We might let the matter go with conventional terms, or hum some current song; he explores nature, science, and myth in search of symbols which will carry his meaning. And he composes his poem with the utmost care for its structure, metrically and otherwise. The five stanzas are highly regular in their rhythm, and each of them strictly honors a pattern of syntax as well as a pattern of rhyme. Each first line begins with "Ask me no more," and each third line with "For." The punctuation almost never varies. The rhyme scheme is the couplet scheme; and yet it is proper that the poem should appear as stanzas, as quatrains, for each set of four lines, with its asking and its answering couplet, is complete in itself, bringing the poem to a pause from which it will start again.

When it starts again, will it be any farther along? Is the poem aiming to be more than a series of statements—five, as it happens, and this is the number of the fingers on the hand that strokes the instrument whence the music comes—strung as stationary beads are strung, one after another on the string? Or is there movement in the whole? Does the poem climb? Does it reach a conclusion? Does it have a climax?

A progression appears if we consider the successive stanzas in terms of the activity, or the amount of activity, each describes. The first stanza, for example, contains no activity at all. Nothing could be quieter than the act, if it is an act, of sleeping in one's cause as the oak sleeps in the acorn or the rose in its seed, its root, waiting patiently to become itself. If this is an act, it must be done in a deep place out of time's reach; for cause itself is not a temporal thing. The place, indeed, is as deep as the lady's beauty, which is an "orient" deep. A famous word, sufficient in itself to have created Carew's reputation. For it suggests many things: the East, the brilliant spaces out of which suns rise, radiance itself, and the more general idea of source or origin—wells or fountains out of which come forth again whatever things have descended into them, or life which can be where death once was. Yet the tangible activity is nil. All is potentiality, and the sweet promise of more in place of less. Nor is the promise lightly stated: Jove is the agent of its fulfilment, and his name alliterates powerfully, decisively, with "June."

The second stanza, breaking the trance of the first, sets things in motion, but small things, and indeed the smallest we can conceive. Atoms of light are finer even than the motes we watch dancing in a sunbeam; yet those motes will do for an image, particularly if we think of them as golden, as gold dust floating. The irregular accents we hear in the word "whither" are in the interest of what now is to be achieved: our sense of irreducible, indivisible, and all but invisible particles of matter set free—"whither do stray"—to wander where they will. Their will, in fact, is to wander toward that place of which their creator was thinking when he ground them up so light and fine. They are to settle upon my lady's already golden hair, where they will be noticed only as perfection is noticed, gracing what once seemed, yet only seemed, to be sufficiently beautiful without it.

The third stanza follows a larger creature to its destination. The nightingale, which sounds as well as is seen—where is its song continued after music's season closes? For such a singer cannot really cease; something must keep her voice warm and sweet, ready to be heard again. And here the poet runs a risk. For his answer, which is that the bird flies into his lady's throat and remains there, could be grotesque or painful if he did not know how to manage the reader's responses. He manages them, among other ways too mysterious to understand, by the word "dividing" and by the alliteration of "winters" with "warm." "Dividing" is a musical term of Carew's century, the seventeenth, and refers to the art of descant, or singing in harmony, or performing in parts. It is a technical term for the miracle by which the many divisions of a song melt finally into one sweet thing, the song itself. The lady's throat, like the whole body of the nightingale, is where music may be said to live, singing for its own pleasure, making sound or no sound as it chooses; wintering, or waiting, in the warmth of its own notes until it chooses to sing so that all may hear. The lady is speaking or singing now; the nightingale will sing in May; but both are the same in idea, and it is in fact idea that entertains us here, not fact, not feathers, not vocal cords, not flesh in any form, nor even any audible sound. Again it is the promise of sound, the certainty that music remains possible, which reassures us after the disappearance of the nightingale. She has not disappeared after all, any more than the flowers of Jove can be said to have died, or the atoms of day to have wandered nowhere.

The fourth stanza reaches far into the universe—a dark universe, too, for now it is the dead of night—and sees the most startling of all movements. Stars fall. And where? Into my lady's eyes, where the quietest of verbs is found for what they do. They "sit," fixed as proper stars are fixed, in the spheres which an old astronomy assumed were there to contain them. These spheres made music, too, grander than that of the nightingale; but the poem, though it lets us think of this, says nothing further about it. Our attention is upon the lady's eyes, which are bright not merely as stars are bright in the conventional comparison, but happy in their brightness because they are the home to which celestial wanderers have come. Once more the image of motion has given way to the image of rest; the moving object has plunged into the medium best fitted to receive it and henceforth to display it.

In the final stanza the mythical phoenix, more potent to our imagination than even the brightest star, plunges also to her rest. But it is not the rest of death. It is a rest after which action will commence again as life recommences in new birth. Nor does it matter where this happens. East or west is immaterial now; we remember "orient" in the third line of the poem, but we are far away from even the remotest east, as we are far away from any west. The phoenix, searching for that spicy place where she can seem to die and yet not die, speeds unerringly to my lady's fragrant bosom, whence she will spring into future flight that contrasts with the quiet power, stated itself so noiselessly in stanza one, exerted by the causes of things. The poem returns to its beginning; draws a circle back through the world of atoms, birds, and stars; and enters, so to speak, itself.

The lady, meanwhile, has not moved, nor has the rhythm of the song abandoned its stateliness, its all but monotonous march of heavy and light syllables, its iambic walk which only in the fifth, seventh, ninth, twelfth, and sixteenth lines shifts momentarily into trochaic. Nor has the singer for one instant relaxed the formality of his smile. He has never become personal. He has kept his mind among metaphysical things, letting science and philosophy do his work of praise. But it was not praise either; it was compliment, which is more intimate and fanciful a thing. The lady never deserved this much. Or did she? The music says she did, and so does the gravity which still lingers in the lover's face. She deserved all that words can say when words refer to the greatest and highest things in the world: immortal things, whose home she is. "Dies" is the last word of the poem, yet death is the last thing it suggests. If any love can last forever, this love will. If any poem can, then this one must.

2. Mary Morison

O Mary, at thy window be,
    It is the wish'd, the trysted hour!
Those smiles and glances let me see,
    That make the miser's treasure poor:
How blythely wad I bide the stour,
    A weary slave frae sun to sun,   5

Could I the rich reward secure,
    The lovely Mary Morison!

Yestreen, when to the trembling string
    The dance gaed thro' the lighted ha',   10
To thee my fancy took its wing,
    I sat, but neither heard nor saw:
Tho' this was fair, and that was braw,
    And yon the toast of a' the town,
I sigh'd, and said amang them a',   15
    "Ye are na Mary Morison."

Oh, Mary, canst thou wreck his peace,
    Wha for thy sake wad gladly die?
Or canst thou break that heart of his,
    Whase only faut is loving thee?   20
If love for love thou wilt na gie,
    At least be pity to me shown;
A thought ungentle canna be
    The thought o' Mary Morison.
                  —ROBERT BURNS

In this love poem there is as much distance between the man who sings and the girl who listens as there was between the lover and the lady of Carew's more elaborate and intellectual song. Or does the girl in this case listen? She is named—three times in the refrain and twice as simply "Mary"—but it is not certain that she hears one word; whereas Carew's lady can be imagined as not only listening but looking, and doubtless smiling at the formal conceits wherewith her beauty is celebrated.

The distance now is measured by a longing for one who perhaps is unattainable. Mary Morison is not yet even at her window. She may never come there; or if she does, she may stand quietly, or sit serenely, giving only half her heed to words she has no intention of answering. Yet it is possible that she will appear, and it is even possible that she loves the singer who desires and misses her so much. Nothing less than the tenderest and sincerest words will test whether this is true. The words of the song must do all that words can do in love's extreme need; they must convince Mary Morison that she is lovable as no other girl is lovable, and they must make it clear that someone is outside her cottage who feels and understands this as no other person could. Music of course would help; but in the absence of an instrument the words must make their own sound, the lines must be their own melody, the stanzas must develop their own effect of extended and considered composition.

The words are Scots words, and there is an advantage in that. The r's are caressingly rolled, and the vowels have a deeper register than English would give them. In the first stanza it is important to note that "hour" rhymes with "poor" and "secure," and of course with the strange word "stour," which stands for the dust, the struggle, the confusion of existence. In the second stanza "hall" and "all" drop their consonant endings so that they may rhyme with "saw" and "braw" (fine, handsome). And in the third stanza "die" and "gie" (give) rhyme with "thee" and "be." It makes a great deal of difference that this is so. The voice of the singer is in consequence not only clear and strong but gentle and concerned; is soft as absolute seriousness is soft, without any suggestion of weakness.

It also makes a great deal of difference that the rhyme scheme is what it is. Each stanza begins with a quatrain, alternately rhymed; and it might be expected, since there are eight lines in each stanza, that a similar quatrain would follow. Such indeed is the case, but instead of a new set of rhymes we hear the sound of the fourth line repeated at the end of the fifth; which means that although the sixth and eighth lines are free to terminate with fresh sounds—and one of these will always be the last syllable of Mary's name—the seventh line must agree with the couplet at the center. But the main thing is that couplet at the center, upon which the stanza pivots. The second of its two lines, surprisingly continuous in sound with the one before it ("stour" with "poor," "braw" with "saw," "gie" with "thee"), has thus an opportunity to express the peculiar earnestness of the singer, who as it were is not willing to let the initial quatrain go without savoring its final note once more. The insistence of the sound is like the insistence of his love. You see, he seems to say, it is really true what I am singing; if my voice rises in this fifth line, and a new energy is heard in it, that is because my love is powerful. My love is a dramatic thing, feeding upon its own thoughts and finding climaxes in the very sounds it utters.

If the middle stanza of the three is more energetic and moving than either of its neighbors, this corresponds with what we have noted—namely, that every stanza is most energetic at its center. The poem, like any good poem, comes in waves; it rises and falls, over all and in its parts. So there is a special fitness in the fact that Burns's middle stanza is his best—his most interesting, his most dramatic, his most persuasive. Each of the three comes to its peak at the proper point, and so does the whole of which they are the parts. The first stanza contents itself with stating the wealth that would be in the singer's hands if Mary were possessed. The third stanza descends into self-pity at the thought that this may never happen—she may never permit herself to be possessed, this gentle girl whom he then implores to respect his longing anyway, to love it if she cannot love him. In the middle stanza, however, he sets his subject in motion; he steps out of the present moment and remembers last night when there was dancing in the lighted hall and he thought of Mary who was not there. As the music sounded and the figures whirled he sat in a trance, contemplating her superiority to every fashionable lady before him. One of them was fair and one of them was fine, and another was the toast of all the town, but none of them was what *she* is. None of them was Mary Morison.

The name itself is enough. To speak it is the only way at last to praise this unique person concerning whom we know nothing except that she is loved by one who when everything else fails can make himself happy by pronouncing two words. She cannot have ungentle thoughts—we know that, or know he hopes so. We know too that she has a window at which she can appear if she will, smiling and glancing. But the one thing we know with conviction and feeling is that he loves her and desires that she love him. The thought of Mary Morison is all we have. It is all *he* has—the lovely Mary Morison, about whom nothing can really be said except that no one else is she. To every other girl alive the poem says: Ye are na Mary Morison. Three times, at the conclusion of three stanzas, the name sings itself with the utmost tenderness, dwelling especially on its own final syllable which the rhythm serves to prolong. But the most telling of these three times is, properly, the second or middle one. It is the proudest, the surest, the most excited. The climax of the poem is where any climax should be: not at the close, but halfway there, with room ahead for afterthought and fullest realization; and, sobering though this may be, for possible sorrow.

3. I Had Not Minded Walls

I had not minded walls
Were Universe one rock,
And far I heard his silver call
The other side the block.

I'd tunnel until my groove   5
Pushed sudden through to his,
Then my face take recompense—
The looking in his eyes.

But 'tis a single hair,
A filament, a law—   10
A cobweb wove in adamant,
A battlement of straw—

A limit like the veil
Unto the lady's face,
But every mesh a citadel   15
And dragons in the crease!
          —EMILY DICKINSON

The beloved person of this poem is unattainable for another reason than that which operated in Mary Morison's case. Mary Morison was attainable whenever she chose to be; she might never so choose, but she was free to make her lover happy; nothing substantial separated them, no third thing outside themselves. In Emily Dickinson's poem there is a third thing, and it will separate two persons forever. The man who is loved can never be reached. Something that seems slight, that indeed is all but invisible, is there between them as big as a mountain, and more rough and hard. It is bigger of course than any mountain; were the entire universe one solid block of rock, this thing would still be greater. The block of rock could be tunnelled through, but this delicate barrier is impregnable. It is convention, it is morality. Or if it is not that—the poem does not give it a name—it is something equally strong. And the business of the poem is to state its strength.

The poem is difficult perhaps. The idea that something in a human mind—or two human minds, or all human minds—may be harder than granite is itself difficult; or it could be to a reader untrained in paradox. But in addition the subject as it exists here is highly personal to the speaker. It is even a secret subject, which she is shy in divulging—shy because it is important, and shy because she is modest. She does not hesitate to confess her own love, but she will not confess for another. The difficulty, such as it is, comes partly from her instinct to protect him; she leaves him unknown to us, as she leaves the subject unknown to all save those who will work it out.

As for him, the beloved person, the first two stanzas come near to suggesting that he is God. In a sense he *is* God, as those greatly loved seem to be. He is too remote and wonder-

ful to possess; he is on the other side of the universe, waiting
to be known; and he can be known only by heroic effort. But
the last two stanzas remove the suggestion. There is no law
against our loving God; the limits interposed between deity
and man are not like these. It is a human situation we have,
and indeed it is all the more tortuous for that. Yet Emily
Dickinson has managed, in the suggestion itself, to deposit in
our minds a feeling that the unattainable person is benign and
blameless—is a great person, to her at any rate, and worthy of
comparison with the greatest Person she knows.

Still she is concealing as much as she can, consistently with
the fact that she speaks at all. She writes so tersely, and wraps
her message so tightly, that we shall miss it unless we listen
close. Her syntax, for example, tends toward oddity; she seems
to leave out necessary words, and she ignores certain rules of
grammar. She is daring us to paraphrase her poem. Yet it is her
desire that we do so, and consequently we shall. A different
and weaker statement will result; but then we shall know what
the force of her utterance was.

"I would not have minded walls between me and the man I
love. If the universe itself were one great wall, as thick as it
was high, and built of solid rock; and if, far around on the
other side of this obstruction, I heard his silver voice calling to
me (or, simply, heard it and knew it was his), then I would
cheerfully tunnel through to where he was. He would have
started too; tunnels are built from both ends, and meet in the
middle; suddenly, therefore, the last bit of rock between us
would be gone, and I would have my reward. My reward,
because the effort was chiefly mine. My tunnel reached his.
Then the reward—my opportunity to look into his eyes. But
this is an idle story. Nothing of the sort ever happened or will
happen. No such opportunity exists. There is no wall, no uni-
versal block between his eyes and mine. Something worse is
there—something as thin as a single hair, a filament; something
as unreal (yet how real!) as a human law. It is as if a cobweb

had been woven out of adamant, the hardest stone; or as if a fortress, though built only with straw, turned out to be more invincible than stone. Something stands between us that looks like nothing at all—a veil, say, on a lady's face. But every part of it is terrible in its power to resist penetration. Suppose it *is* a veil. Well, every mesh of it is a citadel, and every fold of it contains a dragon."

The paraphrase says less than the poem does—so much less that we may learn from the difference what poetry is. The only merit of the prose is that it calls attention to some of the things Emily Dickinson is doing. It accentuates, for instance, her changes of tense. She begins with "I had not," goes on to "I would," and ends in the strict present: "It is." The present fact, the controlling and only fact, is painful; so she has come to it with delays and diversions, pretending for the while that something else was fact. But nothing else was, whereas this *is*. Then there are the suppressed words, the units of grammar and syntax which she forces us to supply. *If the* universe were one rock, and *if* I heard his silver call *on* the other side *of* the block—she does not use the italicized terms, any more than she says in the next stanza: Then my face *would* take recompense. Meanwhile she has written "sudden" for "suddenly," as later on she writes "unto" for "to"—for once a longer word, but this is because it has a more formidable sound than the one we would use in prose, as befits the fact that the situation itself is now absolutely formidable.

What the paraphrase does not do, however, is more significant than what it does. It gives us no sense of the nervous quickness with which Emily Dickinson moves toward the conclusion of her tragic statement. It is not in verse, and it is not in stanzas; nor does it rhyme. Emily Dickinson uses line, stanza, and rhyme to give what she is saying velocity and terror; or, at the end of the second stanza, softness and joy.

> Then my face take recompense—
> The looking in his eyes.

The absence of rhyme between "groove" and "recompense," and the consonance rather than rhyme between "his" and "eyes"—these are bold surprises, even if in the service of an imaginary moment which is not bold at all: two lovers, long separated, are quietly together at last. The failure of perfect rhyme between "walls" and "call" in the first stanza is of another order. The silver call is singular, as it must be, and therefore clear and slender, as the walls are not. So, in the third stanza, the refusal of "adamant" to rhyme with "hair" expresses its implacable hardness. So, in the fourth stanza, "citadel" and "crease" rebel against the law that they repeat the civil music of "veil" and "face." The sound of the long *a* drops suddenly to the sound of short *e* in "every" and "mesh" as well as in "citadel"; and the last line converts it altogether, in the harsh word "dragons" and in the "crease" through which their malevolence can be imagined to hiss. The gentle alliteration in "limit," "like," and "lady" is also gone out of our ears, along with any sense of proportion we might have had permitting us to inquire whether a mesh could ever be a citadel, or dragons inhabit creases.

The stanza looks like a ballad stanza, and yet is not. The first line is short, like the second and fourth; only the third has four feet. The third line in every case is long and full; and each time this has a different function. The drawn-out, lucid silver call; the leisurely taking recompense; the cobweb announcing that it is not silk but adamant, and saying so with special emphasis on the last syllable of that mighty word; the hoarse voice issuing from each mesh of the veil, proclaiming itself, astonishingly and yet convincingly, to be a medieval stronghold—each of these third lines works its own magic, assisting the poem of which it is a part to become one of the most potent in any tongue.

vehicle of simile
tenor & metaphor

4. An Ode

The merchant, to secure his treasure,
   Conveys it in a borrowed name.
Euphelia serves to grace my measure;
   But Chloe is my real flame.

My softest verse, my darling lyre,   5
   Upon Euphelia's toilet lay;
When Chloe noted her desire,
   That I should sing, that I should play.

My lyre I tune, my voice I raise;
   But with my numbers mix my sighs: 10
And whilst I sing Euphelia's praise,
   I fix my soul on Chloe's eyes.

Fair Chloe blushed: Euphelia frowned:
   I sung and gazed: I played and trembled:
And Venus to the Loves around   15
   Remarked, how ill we all dissembled.

                    —MATTHEW PRIOR

Prior's famous little ode takes us back to Carew's song with which we began. They are not the same, but they are alike at one important point. The lover literally sings to his lady, and an instrument accompanies his words. Or so it is in Prior's case at any rate; or so he says. He has a lyre. Carew can be imagined with one, but he does not mention it, entirely occupied as he is with the words he addresses to his listening lady. We do not hear the words of Prior's song to Chloe. We are merely told the story of how he sang them—pretending they were for Euphelia, but intending them for his real flame; and fooling nobody, least of all Venus and her Loves who were looking on, perhaps from the wallpaper, perhaps from a mural which decorated this eighteenth-century chamber, perhaps from the very air; for it was an atmosphere in which the goddess and her Cupids might very well be suspended, half visible, half not, half flesh, half fancy.

It was the atmosphere of gallantry, and gallantry goes by rules. The lover conceals not only the identity of his mistress but the intensity of his feeling for her. His formality is an attempt to sound and look superficial. He is not superficial, but the law of his society demands that he seem so, just as it dresses both him and his lady in wig and ruffle, and powders them like dolls. Every phrase and gesture must be light, and somehow at the same time stiff, as if a dance were being danced, and its elegant figures had been instructed to look as little as possible like human beings.

Prior follows all the rules, and yet his poem is not the frigid thing that each of ten thousand other such poems in its time was then and certainly is now. It has survived its fashion and its age. But not by trying consciously to be different. It is trying to be altogether typical, and in fact succeeding. It is fully realizing the possibilities of its type; and that, no doubt, is the secret of its success with us. Every poem must begin somewhere, must be some kind of poem rather than another, or rather than all others, or rather than none at all. And its chance for immortality may lie in the very fidelity it achieves to its kind. If the fidelity is complete, if the true meaning of the form is found, then the poem becomes true as any other is, no matter what its form or kind. All good poems are different, yet all are alike in being good. Goodness in poems, as in persons, tends to be the same everywhere.

Prior, however, seems to be unaware of this. He begins with a cynical analogy—he deals in matters of love as a merchant deals in matters of cargo and consignment. As the merchant, wishing to make sure that his treasure is safe, labels it with a cheaper name that will tempt no thief to plunder it—cotton instead of gold, or straw instead of cotton—so the hero of the poem (if hero he is) protects the secrecy of his love by pretending in public that someone else is his mistress. Euphelia may not be cheaper than Chloe, but she is not Chloe; and so she will do as the figure he feigns to adore. He addresses his poems to her, he seizes his lyre and sings to her, he encourages people to couple their names; yet all the while it is Chloe whom he loves, as she alone knows (or so he hopes) by the fact that he gazes at her whenever he sings to Euphelia.

The rest of the poem seems to proceed on the same level. Its language is as conventional as Prior can make it. Poetry is "measure" or "numbers," a mistress is a "flame," and the soul of the lover sighs. Also, there is a lyre: the most conventional of instruments, and in a sense the most unreal. There is in fact no lyre, as in fact there is no soul and no attending goddess. Or is this true? Is the poem not passionate, not persuasive? If it is, then the lyre somehow exists, and so does Venus. But Prior seems to be making no effort to convince us. Rather, he is strumming out the most regular tetrameters he can manage; he is keeping his meter mechanical, as if there were no passion for it to convey; and often enough he breaks a line exactly in the middle, leaving two half-lines that bow to each other like figures in a minuet. The fifth, the eighth, the ninth, the thirteenth, and the fourteenth lines—five out of sixteen altogether —are divided in the middle by a knife-sharp caesura, and the two halves thus created are perfectly uniform in grammatical structure. In the fifth line, for example, "softest" balances "darling," and "verse" balances "lyre." So in every case among the five with one exception. In line 13 there is no epithet before Euphelia's name to balance the "fair" before Chloe's; but there could have been none, since Euphelia's name has three syllables. The meter, as we have noted, nowhere is permitted to violate itself. There are precisely eight syllables in every line (ignoring the feminine endings in lines 1, 3, 14, and 16);

the rhymes are perfect; the music is willing to sound monotonous.

Yet it is not monotonous; or if it is, the monotony is powerful. The ode drives on to its end as if its end were important, as indeed it is. For we cannot miss some accent of seriousness here. Perhaps it discloses itself in those five divided lines—especially in the last of them:

I sung and gazed: I played and trembled.

Why the trembling? A cynical lover, willing to use a lady as Euphelia is being used, and in her very house, from her very toilet table, snatching up his lyre to sing a song that will deceive her if it can, and beating out its measure with his voice, his head, his foot—why is he trembling? The reason must be that he loves Chloe very much indeed; that he knows very well what he is doing; that he feels some guilt about Euphelia; that the whole situation has suddenly become tremendous for him —and for the ladies too, who understand this as well as he does, and respectively blush and frown. An artifice has confessed that it is an artifice. The tissue of convention has been torn. A poem that desired to be indistinguishable from ten thousand others has achieved uniqueness, has become comparable with any good poem anywhere. Passion has found its voice. The wigs, the ruffles, the patches, and the powder are forgotten as we realize that these are people like ourselves, trying to live in a set of conventions and—because they are people—failing.

But how has this happened? The poem is short; there would seem to have been too little time for such a development, such a reversal. The answer is not easy to give. There is mystery here as in all successful art. Yet we can remember how early in the ode the bisected line appeared—innocently then, but preparing nevertheless, through three repetitions, for the final instance:

I sung and gazed: I played and trembled.

We can remember too how strong and decisive the accents in each line had been, as if the poem marched somewhere. And now at the end there is Venus, the goddess who hovers over all such scenes when she is deeply concerned with the actors. She must be so concerned in the present case. She has come alive out of the landscape she was in. For she knows what we know—what the verse has made us know—namely, that nobody in love ever fools anybody else. There is a game of gallantry, but its rules are toy things, easily dominated by the law of love. She seems to be saying to her Cupids: "See, dears? They tried well, but they had to fail. My power thrusts through at last. The treasure is not safe. The name was borrowed for nothing. The flame is real indeed." And even so she has not cast off the costume Prior sees her as wearing. She assists in the convention, she encourages the artifice. For she knows that all people must have their conventions, as all poems must have their styles. She can manifest herself in spite of this; or even with its help.

5. To Lucasta, on Going to the Wars

Tell me not, Sweet, I am unkind,
    That from the nunnery
Of thy chaste breast and quiet mind
    To war and arms I fly.

True, a new mistress now I chase,   5
    The first foe in the field;
And with a stronger faith embrace
    A sword, a horse, a shield.

Yet this inconstancy is such
    As thou too shalt adore;   10
I could not love thee, Dear, so much,
    Loved I not Honor more.
         —RICHARD LOVELACE

Perhaps no poet has said more in twelve short lines than Lovelace says in this farewell to his mistress as he leaves her on his way to war—to honorable war, whose claims rival in his feeling, since he is a Cavalier, the claims of love. Once more we have a love poem whose subject is separation; indeed, this is the best subject love has if it will be talking; but Lovelace is not lamenting his necessity to leave. He is justifying it, even exulting in it, and he is counting on Lucasta to understand. She may have called him unkind to go, as the first line suggests; but that is only his cue to speak with all the authority verse can give his voice. The authority sounds in the imperative sentence with which the poem begins.

That it is the authority of intelligence, however, is manifest in the completeness with which the next two lines comprehend the sweetness of the person he is leaving. There may have been gentleness in the fourth word uttered at all, the "Sweet" set off with commas as if a bow or a kiss accompanied it, but lines 2 and 3 can leave no doubt in Lucasta's mind that her lover values the quality in her most opposite to the quality of the experience he now seeks. She is faithful and good, and her spirit is serene. But listen to the verse as it says this.

> That from the nunnery—

the line looks shorter than it is. The ballad stanza of which it is the second line requires that it have three iambic feet, and that it rhyme with the fourth line. It does both things, but only if we stretch out the word "nunnery" as we speak it, and give its last light syllable a fuller emphasis than it normally receives. When we do that—and the stanza makes us do it—we perceive how reluctant the lover is to leave the nest of his happiness. He lingers over the word, which again, since the sense runs on from it into the next line, hangs in the air an instant as if it were unwilling to go the way of other words.

Its essence passes, in fact, into the next line. Without pause and yet without hurry, slowly and most reverently, we hear:

That from the nunnery
Of thy chaste breast and quiet mind—

from all that, what? This remains to be seen, but meanwhile
the third line has made it clear why "nunnery" was used, and
why it was no exaggeration. It is a slow line, mostly monosyllables; and each monosyllable must be deliberately pronounced. Only the "of" and the "and" are unimportant. "Thy
chaste breast"—the reader will be aware that he is being forced
to say "thy" as if its reference were gravely important, and to
say "chaste breast" as if much time had been lovingly allotted
to it. Indeed it is physically impossible to say "chaste breast"
fast. Both words end in sounds that are unintelligible in English unless they are painstakingly articulated, and the sameness
of the sound here makes this doubly true. Another sort of
sameness appears in "quiet" and "mind," two words that open
themselves slowly on the long *i* and remain open, poised there
as "nunnery" was poised at the end of the line before. There
is a recollection in them also of "unkind" that closed line one
on the same sound. They answer the accusation in that word,
suggesting by the very vowel they use, and use so seriously,
that if the lover *is* unkind it is because he has to be, and that
he has counted the cost. He knows what he is leaving, he
knows whom he is being unfaithful to. She is a lady perfect in
virtue and serenity, whose chaste breast and quiet mind are a
whole world, removed from every other world, in which he
would stay if he could.

The poem, poised then once more on "mind," flies swiftly
to the ground for the conclusion of its opening stanza.

To war and arms I fly—

there is the long *i* again, but between it and the sounds it
recalls, and for the first time in the poem thus far, there is
the heavier note of "war and arms." Heavier, not merely because war and arms are in themselves alarming terms, but also
—and Lovelace knows this well—because their vowel is hard

and alien. The nunnery is no more, the chaste breast and quiet mind are already put far behind as the lover goes racing away —almost literally flying—as if to a new mistress who will make him forget this one who watches him go. There indeed he goes, saying the rest of the poem as it were over his shoulder, firmly, and without any further attempt to recapture the tone of lines 2 and 3. They have done their work, but he must now do his.

"True, a new mistress now I chase"—he makes the confession at once, and proceeds to describe her. The stanza in which he does so is the cleverest of the three, and for that reason the poorest, though it is only relatively poor. Cleverness is a fine thing even if it is not the finest. In this case it consists in saying that the mistress is a man—"the first foe in the field." She is the enemy. And this enemy has a forceful front: all three of the key words in line 6 begin with the same letter, the stout letter f. "True"—the beginning word, suggestive of logic and argument, was itself a sign that the speaker intended to make his point by any means available. These are the means; and repetition is another, for the second pair of lines in this stanza says the same thing over: with a still stronger faith than had been proved in lines 2 and 3 of the poem, his embraces are now to be bestowed on a sword, a horse, a shield—impossible things to embrace, particularly the horse, but the exaggeration is consistent with the cleverness. An idea is working now, not a feeling; which again is consistent with the tone of persuasion, that undertakes paradox if it must.

The third stanza returns to the deeper level of the first, though now there is a mixture of feeling and thought. For one thing, Lucasta is addressed again: in the third line another epithet is set off between commas—"Dear," to balance the "Sweet" with which the song began. "Thou too" and "thee"— it is clear that the poet's discourse is once more in the second person. So is it clear that Lovelace is asking Lucasta to think with him and understand him. Her quiet mind is to take in one last paradox. Such a mind is above being interested in cleverness for its own sake, so he will be very serious; still, the statement is one that must be understood by the intellect, and therefore, though with consummate tenderness, he makes it with the last breath he uses.

Yet you too, he says, must adore the inconstancy my second stanza has confessed. Only you, as a matter of fact, *could* adore it. For you are truly extraordinary in being able to comprehend that I could not love you as much as I do if I did not love something else still more than that. I love it more, and you have helped me to do so, because *you* love it as much as you do. One of the reasons I love you—indeed it is the controlling reason—is that distinction in you, that capacity to worship Honor, which has educated me. The qualities of persons are even more important than the persons themselves. Your faithfulness and quietness are still more beautiful than you, being permanent, abstract things. We compliment persons, but we praise qualities; and praise is the greater act, deserved only by the greatest persons. The greatest Person of all we never compliment—how absurd is the very thought. We praise God, and for His qualities of strength and goodness. So with you, for there is in you something still more important and lovable than yourself. It is Honor, which now I am giving every evidence that I love. Therefore you must consent, as I know you do.

The last two lines of the poem say all of that, and as much more as verse is capable of saying when a master uses it. The longest prose paraphrase would still not capture the whole meaning of these justly famous lines. They are famous precisely because they cannot *be* paraphrased.

> I could not love thee, Dear, so much,
> Loved I not Honor more.

There they are, and the statement is complete. So is the poem —one of the briefest masterpieces in the world, and one of the best proofs that poetry can say what nothing else can. A good line of poetry, like any line well and straightly drawn, is the shortest distance between two points. And the two present points are worlds apart: the nunnery, the battlefield.

6.   A Lecture upon the Shadow

Stand still, and I will read to thee
A lecture, love, in Love's philosophy.
   These three hours that we have spent,
   Walking here, two shadows went
Along with us, which we ourselves produced;   5
   But, now the sun is just above our head,
   We do those shadows tread,
And to brave clearness all things are reduced.
   So whilst our infant loves did grow,
   Disguises did, and shadows, flow   10
From us and our cares; but, now 'tis not so.

That love hath not attained the high'st degree,
Which is still diligent lest others see.

Except our loves at this noon stay,
We shall new shadows make the other way.   15
   As the first were made to blind
   Others, these which come behind
Will work upon ourselves, and blind our eyes.
   If our loves faint, and westwardly decline,
   To me thou, falsely, thine,   20
And I to thee, mine actions shall disguise.
   The morning shadows wear away,
   But these grow longer all the day;
   But oh, love's day is short, if love decay.

Love is a growing, or full constant light,   25
And his first minute after noon, is night.
          —JOHN DONNE

A man is talking, not singing, in this poem. He is talking earnestly, to an audience of one, his mistress, and there are no other people in the world; or if there are, and even if they include us, they are irrelevant and worse. They are enemies to the love which is being lectured about; they are shadows which fall upon it and deprive it in some degree of the simple light without which it cannot perfectly live. The lecture is about the danger to this love from shadows. They will be cast from within if cast at all, since flaws in love are self-caused, the work of weakness in the lovers. Donne hopes that no such flaws exist in the love he is considering now, his own love and his lady's, but he is not sure that none does. It may be that no souls are miraculously innocent of shade. It may be that a law of decay operates even between the greatest lovers, a law as inexorable and impersonal as the law of day and night, of sunrise and sunset—the law of nature, which it would take a miracle to defy. He urges his mistress to defy it with him, even as he suggests that they cannot succeed.

The subject is complicated, and the verse expresses this. The two stanzas are followed by simple couplets, but the stanzas themselves are not simple. Each begins with a pentameter couplet; continues with a tetrameter couplet; continues then with a quatrain, internally rhymed, whose third line has only three feet; and concludes with a triplet made up of two lines in tetrameter and one in pentameter. The structure is rigid with respect to rhyme and meter, but free with respect to the distribution of end-stopped and run-on lines. The speaker's voice, intent upon what it is saying, and all but obsessed with the need of precision in the analysis, follows the subject as a hound a hare, in and out of the maze which the lines construct. Lines 3, 4, 10, 16, and 17 run on so radically as almost not to be lines at all. On the other hand there are lines that stop with a jolt when their sense is ended. There are statements like epigrams, and conclusions that have a fatal sound. This is true of the couplets that follow the stanzas and lock them tight; it is equally true of lines 8, 15, 21, and 24. The only thing that matters to Donne is the truth of what he is saying. It is a unique truth, hidden in the unique situation of his love, which is like no other love. Carew, Burns, Prior, and Lovelace could be thought of as singing old themes to the music of familiar instruments, but there is no line of melody here, and certainly no instrument other than Donne's voice, which beats out its message with a fierce seriousness, and spares no syllable an accent if the sense requires it. The pronouns—"We ourselves" in line 5, "ourselves" and "our" in line 18, "me" and "thine" in line 20, and "I," "thee," and "mine" in line 21—are personal to the utmost degree, and heavily stressed: so stressed, indeed, that the lines are unreadable unless we feel accent falling upon them as if a weight descended. Or as if a finger, admonishing the listener, struck time as well as meaning. You see, someone is saying, this is the way it is; listen closely, and use all your mind, or you will not understand; and not to understand would be to lose everything.

The lecture is in love's philosophy, and we should remember that for Donne the word "philosophy" meant among other things what we mean by "science." The possible faults this love of theirs may commit, the weaknesses it is naturally heir to, are internal faults and weaknesses, but analogies may be found in the external world that mathematics and astronomy deal with. The whole poem, in fact, develops one analogy, and seems to develop it so carefully that we might think a diagram of it could be drawn. Ignoring the analogy for a moment, we may notice what the poem says concerning the love in question. It is perfect only now. While it was growing to this perfect point, it was flawed by the fact that the lovers, instead of contemplating only each other, contemplated other persons: in their need to be secret, they were diligent lest others know that their love existed. This was necessary, but it diverted some of love's energy from its proper object, which is itself. Now, however, that necessity is past. But can their love continue perfect? For a new danger suddenly presents itself. Having learned to protect themselves from others, they may henceforth practice the art between their two selves; some disguise, some lack of candor, some deception, even, may continue to detract from the purity of their mutual gaze. The chief trouble is that love, like any other growing thing, is also a dying thing, and holds in perfection, as Shakespeare says, only for a moment. Can their love live past this present moment of its peak? He hopes it can, yet fears that it cannot. Nothing else could.

And here the analogy comes in. A day is perfect only at the mathematical moment of noon. All morning it was becoming, and all afternoon it is passing away. At the instant of noon it is complete, and there are no shadows; but noon cannot last. The earth is already turning down—the sun is beginning to decline—and there is no way to stop this. Nor is there any comfort, necessarily, in the fact that the afternoon will be long. It *is* afternoon, and there is no escaping that. The day is dying; is in a sense already dead, since it is not perfect any more. Light, like love, is absolute. All or nothing is its law.

So Donne follows a day through its career, and finds it, except for the mathematical moment of noon, dark with shadows. It is like their love, which only now is whole. They can imagine that they have been walking since sunrise, making shadows that correspond to the diligence of all lovers "lest others see." Now at noon they stand on their shadows and everything is clear; but unless noon can last longer than the moment allotted to it, they will begin to make another pair of shadows, corresponding to those deceptions and disguises which stain even the most durable love; they will blind not others but themselves, and then their love will be in some sense dead. Not in one sense, for it has a long afternoon before it. But absolutely, yes. The first minute after noon is night.

The analogy is not faultless, and perhaps no such analogy could be. Science does not assist poetry as much as Donne seems to have thought it could. How can shadows, which lie flat on the ground, with no elevation or thickness, "blind" anybody? Shadows are not disguises, no matter how they lie. And which way are the lovers walking? Presumably from east to west, with the sun; in which case, if their shadows *could* prevent others from seeing them, there indeed they would be, preceding them over the earth's surface, perhaps as substitute images thrown out to divert the public gaze. Well enough. But now for the afternoon. Assuming that progress is straight ahead, shadows will fall behind, and so the poem says in line 17. But in that case how can they blind the lovers? They will not be seen at all, except by others who look after the departing pair.

The diagram we started to draw, in other words, cannot be finished; the analogy does not work. Faults within us are shadows if one likes—it is an acceptable metaphor—but when they are identified with the shadows of morning and evening we fail beyond a point to understand. Not that this matters. And not that it matters if we find ourselves asking what utility there is in a lecture which urges the impossible. Does our lover really believe he will succeed? He seems to, and then again he seems not to—he seems indeed to take a perverse pleasure in denying that there is any hope. For he has seized, to illustrate his homily, something that inevitably and naturally fails. The sun cannot be stopped. Day cannot be prevented from dying.

All we have is a wonderful, rich poem, intricate at its center beyond our power to parse its statement. Perhaps we should not try to parse it. The meaning is clear and terrible enough. "Stand still." Here it is. "Oh, love's day is short, if love decay." No analogy had been needed to support this, yet we should not be sorry for the attempt to find one. For we have noted a unique seriousness in the man who searched it out. He is like no other poet, and doubtless like no other man. Yet he is a man, or else we could not know that he is right when he

concludes, with no matter how much of his confusion unre-
solved:

> Love is a growing, or full constant light,
> And his first minute after noon, is night.

7. Bathsheba's Song

Hot sun, cool fire, tempered with sweet air,
Black shade, fair nurse, shadow my white hair.
Shine, sun; burn, fire; breathe, air, and ease me;
Black shade, fair nurse, shroud me and please me;
Shadow, my sweet nurse, keep me from burning,   5
Make not my glad cause cause of mourning.
> Let not my beauty's fire
> Inflame unstaid desire,
> Nor pierce any bright eye
> That wand'reth lightly.   10
>   —GEORGE PEELE

An early Elizabethan play, *The Love of King David and
fair Bethsabe*, commences with this song. The heroine, whom
we more commonly know as Bathsheba, sings it as she bathes
on the roof of her house while King David watches from a
window of his. She is not aware that he watches, and naturally
does not dream of the consequences. Peele's play, like the Old
Testament from which he took his story, goes on to deal with
the consequences. David falls in love with Bathsheba, arranges
for her husband to be killed in battle, and after suitable punish-
ment for his crime is permitted by God to take her as his queen.
But here we are not concerned with the consequences. Bathsheba, bathing on her roof in sun and shadow, simply sings of
the fear she feels lest some man's eye behold her; and the
shadow she invokes, unlike the fatal shadows in Donne's poem,
is to protect and save her. The love of King David and fair
Bathsheba has not yet begun; when it is on its way to noon,

Donne's poem may apply. Not now, however, when the sun of love is only about to rise.

The song is an incantation whose very phrases caress themselves. Bathsheba, softly conscious of her beauty, takes exquisite pleasure in the elements that in her imagination minister to it. The hot sun, cool at this distance and yet a great fire which could consume her if it wished, is tempered by sweet currents of free air that bathe her as much as the water does, or the oils and perfumes which doubtless assist the process. These things are all about her, tangibly serving her delight and making her happy enough to sing. But there is one more element she feels and sees, and it is the most important one. Black shade is her fair nurse, capable of shielding her from the danger that is deepest in her mind. There is the danger of being consumed by the sun, and shadows can prevent that; but better yet, they can keep her from burning because her beauty is so irresistible—to herself, and to others. As she is conscious of this beauty, so some bright eye may be. Unstaid, unchecked desire, in herself, in *him*, stands ready to be born. We should not inquire whether her fear is real, her modesty unmixed. She says what she says, and our business is to listen, trying as we do so to explain the peculiar effectiveness of her song.

The words, for one thing, tend all to have equal power. The rhythm is slow and luxurious, delighting in its own full movement from syllable to syllable, as if every syllable were accented. The poem can, if one wishes, be read differently; can be read rapidly, with a pronounced trochaic emphasis. Thus in the first line there can seem to be only four accents—on "Hot," "cool," the first syllable of "tempered," and "air." And so on through the five lines that follow. But then a great deal that is important will have been suppressed. A slower reading will discover seven accents—in line one, on every syllable except "with" and the second syllable of "tempered." The spondaic movement thus revealed is more convincing, for it goes with the meditation we hear in Bathsheba's voice: meditation upon herself, considered part by part, deliciously. Or still another system of accents might be found. Perhaps it does not matter how many there are, in this song that sings itself as if it did not know we were listening, and says only what is true to its own genius.

"Make not my glad cause cause of mourning." The last of the long lines is more complex than the rest, though it is not especially difficult. The two "causes" require that we listen closely and think a little, as Bathsheba is thinking. Presumably she means: Make not the cause that I am glad (my beauty) become the cause that I shall mourn. The four short lines that follow—two couplets, quickly disposing of the subject that three longer ones have developed—go on to sketch the content of this serious possibility. It is only sketched, but we do not feel its force any the less for that. The meter is now iambic beyond a doubt; yet even here it wantons with irregularity.

> Let not my beauty's fire
> Inflame unstaid desire.

Nothing could be more formally iambic than this trimeter couplet, which by its very decorum seems to have conquered danger. But the next little line is not so easy to scan. Does the *y* in "any" have no accent? Does "bright"? And the last line of all—it goes with the wind. There are only five syllables, and two of them, the third and fifth, are so light as to be almost weightless. Like Bathsheba's thought, that wandereth. And lightly, as the song whispers to its close.

8. They Flee from Me

I

They flee from me that sometime did me seek,
With naked foot stalking *with*in my chamber.
Once have I seen them gentle, tame, and meek,
That now are wild, and do not *once* remember

That sometime they *have* put themselves in danger   5
To take bread at my hand; and now they range,
Busily seeking *in* continual change.

One especial time:

Thanked be fortune it hath been otherwise,
Twenty times better; but once especial,
In thin array, after a pleasant guise,   10
When her loose gown *did from her shoulders* fall,
And she me caught in her arms long and small,
And therewith*al* so sweetly did me kiss
And softly said, Dear heart, how like you this?

It was no dream, *for* I lay broad *a*waking.   15
But all is turned *now*, through my gentleness,
Into a *bitter* fashion of forsaking;
And I have leave to go, of her goodness,
And she also to use newfangleness.
But since that I *unkindly so* am served,   20
How like you this? what hath she *now* deserved?

II

They flee from me that sometime did me seek,
With naked foot stalking in my chamber.
I have seen them gentle, tame, and meek,
That now are wild, and do not remember
That some time they put themselves in danger   5
To take bread at my hand; and now they range,
Busily seeking with a continual change.

Thanked be fortune, it hath been otherwise
Twenty times better; but once, in speciall,
In thin array, after a pleasant guise,   10
When her loose gown from her shoulders did fall,
And she me caught in her arms long and small.
Therewith all sweetly did me kiss,
And softly said, Dear heart, how like you this?

It was no dream; I lay broad waking. 15
But all is turned, thorough my gentleness,
Into a strange fashion of forsaking;
And I have leave to go of her goodness,
And she also to use newfangleness.
But since that I so kindely am served, 20
I fain would know what she hath deserved.
                                 —SIR THOMAS WYATT

An accident of history has made this poem even more interesting than it would otherwise be. It would be interesting in any case, but we may learn a great deal from the fact that it exists in two forms. In the form first given here it was famous for three and a half centuries; it is still more famous in its second form, unknown until a few decades ago. The second form is Wyatt's own, and therefore the first in fact; but the other was the first to be printed, and the only one that could be read until the author's manuscript was studied. The person responsible for I was Richard Tottell, an anthologist who in 1557 published a celebrated *Miscellany*, and who "improved" this poem before he put it in print. He seems to have believed that Wyatt was ignorant of versification. The poem was intended to be in iambic pentameter; so Tottell made sure that the intention was carried out—to his ear, anyway.

The ear of Tottell was not satisfied by an apparent shortage of syllables in lines 2, 3, 4, 5, 13, 15, 17, and 21. The shortage was real by the metronome, for by count there is a syllable missing in each of those lines. Tottell's additions to cure the malady are italicized in the present text. They supply what was never there, and ruin the rhythm Wyatt achieved. Wyatt knew what he was doing when he wrote, for instance:

With naked foot stalking in my chamber.

The missing syllable between "foot" and "stalking" causes the line to *stalk*, as the pronoun "I" at the beginning of the next line, naked of any sound before it, assumes the importance it

· 35 ·

has for him who uses it. The experience of the poem is not only personal, it is unique; and it is communicated to us with a bewildered sense of strangeness—it could not be, yet it is. So the "I" here needs to be naked, for the same reason that "once" in line 4 would be gratuitous. "*And* do not remember"—we are forced then to accent the "and," as if we understood: "*And,* mind you!" The speaker is very serious, and so prolongs certain syllables in his speech, for emphasis and to make us comprehend not merely his meaning but the uniqueness of it, and possibly the enormity. Tottell's "have" in line 5 prevents us from hearing the italics in "some" which Wyatt surely heard. "*Some* time—oh, not now, but I tell you it was true *then.*"

When Tottell came to line 7, the last in its stanza, he found Wyatt in what he thought was the opposite error: he had put in an extra syllable. Wyatt had done this so that we might have a sudden sense of coming and going, hither and yon, on the part of those who do not come to him any more. The stanza as he wrote it ran away as they had run, in a light chaos of syllables and feet. So in line 9, though there was nothing wrong with the number of sounds, Tottell appears to have thought that "especial" was smoother than "in speciall" set off with commas. But Wyatt had wanted emphasis there, not smoothness; he was about to describe the remarkable thing that happens, or happened, in this stanza. What happened was that a lady came, in a thin loose gown, and the gown fell from her shoulders as she caught him and kissed him. Wyatt's eleventh line keeps the gown on as long as it can, then lets it fall abruptly, even awkwardly, in the words "from her shoulders did fall." Tottell, all for smoothness, transfers the "did" to its place in the natural word order; and the fall becomes ordinary. "Therewith," writes Wyatt at the beginning of line 13, "all sweetly did me kiss"—that is to say, very sweetly, or completely so. But Tottell returns to the normal range by writing "And therewithal."

Line 15 suffers as much as any line in the poem from the

blacksmith's hand that hammered it out longer. "It was no dream," insists Wyatt, though you may think so; I tell you, and you must believe it, "I *lay broad wak*ing." Each of the italicized syllables demands to be heard, even though in this case there will be only eight syllables in the entire line. Tottell makes it ten, and goes on in line 16 to supply an unnecessary "now" before "through," which for Wyatt had been "thorough"—an older form, more suitable in the environment of "my gentleness," and more effective because no syllable intrudes between it and "turned." The change of "strange" to "bitter" in the next line was of a more radical sort, since it altered the meaning. But Tottell, eager to get in his tenth syllable, may not have thought it mattered; or may not have thought the meaning *was* changed. Wyatt could have thought "bitter," but he wrote "strange"—a term of understatement, introducing irony. The irony in line 20 was stronger still. Of course Wyatt meant "unkindly," as Tottell blunderingly makes clear. But he wrote "kindely," a word of three syllables which made the line complete even for such as Tottell. It was not smoothly complete, however, so the improver said "unkindly so," making sure that we should miss the mockery in Wyatt's little syllable "*e*." Something like the same thing was done to the last line, which Wyatt must have meant to be heard slowly, as if it were spoken with a drawl, the pronoun "she" coming in of course for special emphasis. Tottell's bright question at the beginning of the line is much too bright; and there is that nonsensical "now" for which nothing but a metrical excuse can be offered.

Wyatt's meter was perfect as it stood. The time of each line was right, however many syllables had been suppressed. When a syllable was missing, another one, or several others, pronounced themselves slowly enough to make up the difference. Tottell might have heard this as we do, and admired the result. But Tottell did not know how important verse is to poetry. Verse is not the same thing as poetry, but it makes poetry become the thing it is—the spoken, the individual thing which someone wants to say and have understood in its own terms and no others. Even with Tottell's tampering the poem is distinguished, and for a long time was thought so by those who did not know what had been done to it. It is now more beautiful because it is more itself. It has its own voice, in which it tells a tale that is true only of him who speaks, and of his lady.

What would the tale be if anybody else told it? If we did, for instance? Two lovers have become free of each other, and one of them confesses how it happened. "Thorough my gentleness," he says, "I let it happen. I do not know precisely how, but there it is. We are both free now to go where we please. I am free, I know, because something that used to be true for me is not true any more. When I was bound to my lady I had strange dreams. Or were they dreams? At any rate, my chamber was visited and inhabited by—what were they, girls? Dreams of girls? Animals, padding on their naked feet? Cats? Leopards? People? I am too confused to say, now that my mind is clear. I wish it were not so clear. I knew what they were then, even if I could not have named them. I did not need to name them. They were the signs of my bondage—and, by a paradox of love, they were symbols of my wealth, even of my freedom. For though I am said to be free now, I do not feel free. I can go anywhere, but I do not wish to start. I am supposed to be happy, as she tells me she is, but I do not feel happy. Newfangleness—that is all either of us has, and it is a slight thing, well expressed by its absurd name. I know what my reward is, for gently indulging this fashion of infidelity that now is fixed in our society. My reward is nothing. My lady was curious, and wanted to try the fashion out. Well, then, what is *her* reward? I fain would know. That is all I have to say."

But this is a poor telling, and a wordy one. Wyatt used the fewest possible words, as good poets always do. He used too few, thought Tottell, who sprinkled others in. Yet Tottell could not touch the central mystery of the poem, nor can we in any paraphrase. The mystery of the poem is partly inherent in its subject and partly a creation of Wyatt's words—dark words, delivered with an authority that makes itself heard in every sound the lines make. The lines make their own music —muted by Tottell, but surviving even him—and in the last analysis express themselves.

9. The Soul Selects Her Own Society

The soul selects her own society,
Then shuts the door;
On her divine majority
Obtrude no more.

Unmoved, she notes the chariot's pausing   5
At her low gate;
Unmoved, an emperor is kneeling
Upon her mat.

I've known her from an ample nation
Choose one;   10
Then close the valves of her attention
Like stone.

—EMILY DICKINSON

If this is a love poem, it has at least one thing in common with those we have been discussing. Indeed, it generalizes them. Love annihilates or ignores all persons in the world save one. For the lover in Carew's song there was only one lady—the things he claimed for her could not have been true for more than just that one. For Burns there was not even the possibility of comparison between Mary Morison and any other girl. None of them was she, and that was final. In Emily Dickinson's own poem, "I Had Not Minded Walls," a single silver call was

imagined from the far side of the universe. Prior's ode set
Chloe off against Euphelia—a secret diamond, difficult for even
its setting to reveal. Lovelace, saying farewell to Lucasta, told
her that only an abstraction was holier than she. Donne's drama
confined two lovers in a world uniquely theirs. Peele's Bathsheba had only a potential lover in mind, but his wandering
bright eye would be his and his alone. Wyatt's dream—and yet
it was no dream—was of a particular lady, with arms long and
small. So, Emily Dickinson returns to say, the truth about all
this can be distinctly stated. The soul selects her own society:
it chooses one.

The statement is distinct indeed. The march of these lines
is like the march of doom, with every so often a heavy down-
beat, as if another mile of fate had been measured. Every other
line is short, and ends with a conclusive term, a monosyllable
whose authority is not to be questioned. The preceding line in
each case has been longer; has had a feminine ending; and has
needed this line to complete its statement. Only in one case,
the first, was there punctuation; even there, after "society,"
the comma might have been dispensed with, though the initial
proposition would then have been less striking than it is. However, "Then shuts the door" sets the pattern for all of the five
short lines to follow. "Obtrude no more" is a command delivered in the same tone, and itself shuts a door, as also it opposes
to the light sounds of the preceding line the heavy sounds it
carries thus far, then drops. "Divine majority" is interesting
not only because of its paradox—the majority is one person—
but equally because of the musical contrast it makes with
"obtrude" and "no more." This is an immediate echo of what
had happened in lines 1 and 2. The alliteration of *s*'s in "soul,"
"selects," and "society" seemed for a moment to be answered
by "shuts," but the eventual result was different in the extreme.
"The door"—not "a door," or "her door," but "*the* door," the
only door there is for souls and queens.

The middle stanza, like the middle stanza of "Mary Morison," particularizes and dramatizes the subject. The soul is seen in the act of refusing admission to any other person than the one selected. Unmoved—twice we hear the word—she notes a new candidate, and ignores him. He is an emperor, as she is a queen. But he cannot come in. He is even denied the dignity of a rebuke. She sits unmoved, waiting for him to ride on in his chariot. It has paused at her low gate—her mansion is a humble one, distinguished only by its inhabitant—and the emperor, who has descended, kneels upon her mat. Not upon a pavement of gold or pearls, for nothing like that is there, but upon a common door mat such as plain houses have; the difference is heard in the imperfect rhyme, the flat consonance, the utter refusal of "mat" to be imposing. But in any case she is unmoved. The repetition of that word is curiously powerful. The grammar too is curious. It cannot be the emperor who is unmoved—quite the contrary, for he is moved by desire to enter where she is. Yet the grammar says so, and cares not if it does. Or rather it prefers to do so, for it is lofty like the lady of whom it speaks, and if it wishes to be illicit it will. It is its own law, as she, the unmoved and unmovable, is her own judge of whom she will consent to admit. Not him, not anybody else now. The door is shut, and the divine majority of one—of two—is established forever.

If there had been any question in stanzas 1 and 2 about the number of admitted persons, stanza 3 makes it abundantly clear. Perhaps there was a question—it may be possible for the soul to select a numerous society, or at any rate a few, not one. Certainly it is possible, since all things are possible to such a queen. But what are the facts? "I've known her"—this is the fact, in a certain case anyway. The most interesting case, and doubtless the typical one. "I've known her from an ample nation"—many people, many candidates, an army of them, a world of them—"choose one." Again the grammar is strange. "*To* choose one" is what we should normally say. But the preposition would weaken the infinitive, and so it is cast out.

Two words, distinctly spoken, are enough now for each of the short lines in this final stanza. For the stanza must be final indeed. The short lines above had two accents, but used more than two words. Now two will do. "Choose one"—each word is said hard, said deliberately. "Like stone"—and again it is true, though now with double effect, for we are forced in addition to consider how valves could in any sense be like stone. Are they the valves of the heart? Of the mind? Does attention have valves at all? And if so, is it possible to understand "Like stone"? There is really no question. The last line carries its own authority. Such a thing, so said, has to be true. All of the *n*'s in the stanza come to their climax in the ultimate word, as "valves" had matched "ample" in its vowel, the only open one anywhere in four remarkable lines. Elsewhere the utterance is stern and close-lipped, as if the last thinkable thing were being said. Perhaps in some terrible sense it was.

For there is terror in the fact this brilliant poem discloses. Its first editor called it "Exclusion," for the natural reason that solitude is its subject. A solitude of two, but merciless nevertheless. This door will never be opened again. Attention's valves, whatever soft material they were originally made of, are to be stone throughout eternity.

10.   A Noiseless, Patient Spider

A noiseless, patient spider,
I mark'd, where, on a little promontory, it stood, isolated;
Mark'd how, to explore the vacant, vast surrounding,
It launch'd forth filament, filament, filament out of itself;
Ever unreeling them—ever tirelessly speeding them.   5

And you, O my Soul, where you stand,
Surrounded, surrounded, in measureless oceans of space,
Ceaselessly musing, venturing, throwing—seeking the
     spheres, to connect them;

Till the bridge you will need, be form'd—till the ductile
  anchor hold;
Till the gossamer thread you fling, catch somewhere, O
  my Soul.   10
                    —WALT WHITMAN

Here is solitude with a vengeance, in vacancy so vast that any soul seen at its center, trying to comprehend and inhabit it, looks terribly minute. Whitman's spider on its little promontory—a twig, a stalk, a leaf of grass—is no more helpless than the soul of a man must be, laboring to launch itself in the universe and connect the spheres; or even to catch anywhere, at one fact, one friend, one lover, and thus no longer be alone. Emily Dickinson's soul had the society of one person, and was content with that one. Here there are no persons yet—only the soul newborn in space, hoping to conquer its measureless environment.

The verse of the poem is free, yet not altogether so. It is bound to the task of saying for the poet how strenuous the effort is he has set himself to describe. It arranges itself in two sections—hardly stanzas, though they are almost that—and keeps a certain symmetry in those sections, a symmetry consistent with the parallel Whitman wants to maintain between the spider and the soul. After a relatively short line, each section throws out four longer ones. These have five, six, or seven stresses as the case may be; but they are roughly uniform in the time they take and in the nature of their movement. Their movement is the movement of throwing, of putting out, of launching forth filaments of themselves, of sending loops and spirals into space. "Ever unreeling them—ever tirelessly speeding them." This expresses the poem as well as the spider. Short as it is, it never seems to be done, except in so far as the last line promises some sort of success, somewhere, sometime. The soul, as if it were itself a spider, has put forth gossamer threads. One of them—the suggestion is clear—may catch.

The two adjectives in the first line are more cunning than we may suspect. Their order is eloquent of the creature referred to—not a patient, noiseless spider, but one whose silence strikes us first, and then its industry. In another poem Whitman has spoken, not of the few large stars that glorify the night, but of "the large few stars." The difference is wonderful, as it is here. And the spider has the whole of the beginning line to itself, as if there were no observers. But there is one. "I mark'd." There, on its little promontory, says Whitman, "it stood isolated." And then he marked how it had work to do, how it strove to overcome its isolation, its immense isolation in the space between the twig it clung to and any other object whatever. Not only did it feel out with its arching, delicate feet; from its very self it sent out filament, filament, filament—more and more of them all the time, as if it contained infinities of thread—in search of something with which contact could be made and a web begun. "Filament," used three times in precisely this place, becomes a more forceful word than we could have supposed it would be. It is a light word, like the thing it names; but the three f's fill it with an energy which does not leave us surprised when we learn in the next line that the spider never became tired. The filaments went forth fast, too—faster and faster, and farther and farther away. Nothing could be compared with this. Nothing, except the soul.

My own soul, says Whitman, stands in the same fashion, surrounded by the same sea of vacancy. Or seas—or oceans, a better word—of empty air. The sentence he addresses to this essence of himself is never completed. The sentence about the spider was in the past tense and described an action; the action was not completed, but the observation of it was, and so the sentence could be. But the second half of the poem hangs unfinished, unconnected, in syntax, time, and space. *This* is the situation *now*. The soul keeps on, ceaselessly, throwing out filaments of itself—thoughts, theories, desires—and will do so forever until the day when contact is made with that reality which is as far away as the stars in their spheres. Such a day will undoubtedly come, but it has not come yet. There is not merely the hope that it will come, there is the purpose and the certainty; and somehow we are assured of this by the sound of the last five words in line 9. "Till the ductile anchor hold" —the moment is forecast with an authority we cannot question, since the thing itself is happening in our eyes and ears. Particularly our ears. The hard c's in "ductile" and "anchor" verify the competence of the one filament that is successful at last; it is flexible, but it is strong, and it will *hold;* the merest gossamer, it will nevertheless catch (another hard c) and stay caught. The near-rhyme of "Soul" with "hold" already commences the operation of sewing and tying the anchor tight.

The effort, meanwhile, has been immense. It is an ancient idea, this of man's mind or soul that in its little sphere of flesh can achieve a correspondence with the great sphere of creation around it. And there have been times when this correspondence was spoken of as easy to bring about—indeed, it almost happened by itself. Not so with Whitman, whose modern soul was haunted by the difficulties of the task. Whitman studied loneliness like a scholar, and made his various music out of solitude, his great subject. Here his music is urgent and anxious. The spider and the soul may fail. And yet they may not—indeed they must not, as the rolling energy of the verse by its own might declares. And as the adjectives, so intelligently and powerfully placed, assure us if we listen well. Not only "noiseless" and "patient," but "vacant" and "vast," and "ductile," and "gossamer," which stitches the sections together, giving us to understand that as the spider is assisted by the very genius for survival that can be assumed in its species, so the soul must be similarly assisted, though Whitman does not know how. Yet "somewhere, O my Soul."

11. The Garden

Free Verse

Like a skein of loose silk blown against a wall
She walks by the railing of a path in Kensington Gardens,
And she is dying piece-meal of a sort of emotional anemia.

And round about her there is a rabble
Of the filthy, sturdy, unkillable infants of the very poor.   5
They shall inherit the earth.

In her is the end of breeding.
Her boredom is exquisite and excessive.
She would like someone to speak to her,
And is almost afraid that I will commit that indiscretion.   10

delgira

—EZRA POUND

The skein of loose silk which this lady is, or looks to be, may
remind us of Whitman's filaments and gossamer threads. But
we shall note more differences than resemblances. For one
thing, the silk has made contact with something—a wall—and
this has come about through the lady's weakness. She has
merely been blown against the world, where she clings help-
lessly, not knowing why she is there. Also, she did not launch
forth the loose silk. She *is* the loose silk; the contact has been
involuntary. She has no will. She is dying from lack of it, and
from the emotional anemia that accompanies her sickness as a
symptom. Her sickness is boredom, is ignorance of why she
lives. She will certainly not reproduce herself, as the mothers
and fathers of poor children do—as the parents of these unkillable infants about her have done. She scarcely understands
why they did so, or why anyone should. She is rich, over-bred,
and hopelessly effete. There is only one thing she can do. "She
walks by the railing of a path in Kensington Gardens"—the
very rhythm of the line sets her going there, tall and graceful,

· 46 ·

swaying in the London wind, uncertain as to why or whither she goes. A hesitating step, or perhaps a full stop now and then, suggests that she might enjoy being spoken to—a *human* contact. Yet it is immediately clear that she would not like this either. She is almost afraid that the only person looking at her now, the poet himself, will commit that indiscretion. For it would be an indiscretion. And worse yet, she would have nothing to say.

Her solitude is wittily created in ten lines which trail off thus, leaving her with her little fears lest indiscretion occur. The ten lines, separated into three short sections of three, three, and four, maintain a relaxed movement, a flat tone, so consistent with their subject that we actually hear them in the process of creating it. The bold, circular, stressful movement of Whitman's poem is quite gone, and indeed would have been out of place in this one. This one takes place at the end of time—her time, anyway, and the time of all such people. They are bred beyond purpose, and beyond desire. The traditional idioms of poetry are too good for them, and so will not be used. "A sort of emotional anemia"—a diagnosis is being made, in medical prose. The idiom of detached statement comes suddenly in at this point, after two and a half lines which might have seemed to be pointing in another direction. The simile that fills the first line, and the rhythm of the second —these break off and something else begins. The rest of the poem will be in a new style, a dry, analytical, faintly contemptuous style which suits Pound's view of the matter. He has a human specimen before him, and he proceeds to dissect it.

The lines of free verse are long, but the effect is of clipped, unfeeling sentences, spoken tonelessly in sequence. Lines 6, 7, and 8 are complete sentences, and indeed they are the shortest ones in the poem; but they are somehow typical. The whole poem is trying to sound like prose—a series of declarative sentences with no pretensions to being anything save true. There is a total absence of meter, and an apparent indifference to rhythm. But rhythm is there, and it is organized; and so we have a poem.

The rhythm is organized both within and between the sections, each one of which differs interestingly from the other two. The first, in somewhat willowy lines, unfurls the subject for us to see—the lady walking, and incidentally dying as she walks. The third section settles firmly into the matter-of-fact mood which the subject has turned out to deserve.

> In her is the end of breeding.
> Her boredom is exquisite and excessive.

The genius of "exquisite and excessive" is the genius of prose. Pound is paying no attention to the supposed law of poetry that *s*'s and *ks*'s in concentration should be avoided as difficult and ugly. He piles them on, because the words containing them say exactly what he wants to say; and in the same dogged spirit makes his two diagnostical announcements, each one of them closing its sense where the line closes. Then the trailing off in the two final lines—the poet is already losing interest; perhaps is looking away in search of a better subject.

Meanwhile the middle section, of which little has so far been said—what should be said of that? As with Burns, Lovelace, and Emily Dickinson, it is the heart section, the dramatic section, of the work. Without it we should scarcely have a poem; or at any rate we would have one that did not move. Here for contrast is a world of figures about the central one, the lady who is possibly not worth describing. They make her so, for the purposes of satire at any rate. They are the infants of the very poor, and they do not know that there can be a life like hers. Theirs is the life of the swarm, whose hum is heard in the energy with which lines 4 and 5 are written. "*R*ound about her there is a *r*abble"—the alliteration introduces an alien force, as the word "rabble" itself names a thing which to the lady must be shocking. At this point she seems herself to become aware of the incomprehensible urchins who infest her park, her garden. The remarkable series of adjectives in line 5 is her series as well as Pound's. In so far as they are his they may be understood as somehow hurled at her in derision, or anyhow in explanation of the unfortunate isolation she moves in. She has no energy, but they are energy itself. The suggestion is that she knows and feels this too. "Filthy, sturdy, unkillable"—the crescendo is wrathful if it is hers, and all the more so because it is desperate. "Unkillable" is not humorous for her as it is for Pound and us. It refers to a fact. These are the meek who shall inherit the earth. Some of them are killable as individuals, but the mass is not. Her kind can go out—is going out now—but these we shall have with us always. It is as if she set her lips and said it: "filthy, sturdy, unkillable infants of the very poor."

Then she remembers: "Shall inherit the earth." The section ends as she does so, and the next one continues in the tone thus set. There is nothing she can do now. It might cure her to talk with some living person. That poet, for example, who stands there staring at her. But no; manners forbid it. So she winds on down the path, barrenly triumphant over indiscretion. Her manners, exquisite and excessive, have prevailed; she will die as she has lived, if being like this is living at all.

Free verse as good as Pound's in this poem, and as different from Whitman's in "A Noiseless, Patient Spider," is more difficult to manage than many readers know. The penalty in case of failure is a flatness, a tameness which the mind will not tolerate. The reward of success, on the other hand, is very high. Naturalness is the end all art desires. There are numerous ways of reaching it, and free verse is only one of them. But it is as good as any when wit works through it as it has worked through the words and lines of *The Garden*. No word, no line here could be changed without changing the poem. Anyone who doubts this might make the experiment.

12. The Solitary Reaper

Behold her, single in the field,
  Yon solitary Highland lass!
Reaping and singing by herself;
  Stop here, or gently pass!
Alone she cuts and binds the grain,   5
And sings a melancholy strain;
O listen! for the vale profound
Is overflowing with the sound.

No nightingale did ever chaunt
  More welcome notes to weary bands   10
Of travelers in some shady haunt,
  Among Arabian sands:
A voice so thrilling ne'er was heard
In spring-time from the cuckoo-bird,
Breaking the silence of the seas   15
Among the farthest Hebrides.

Will no one tell me what she sings?—
  Perhaps the plaintive numbers flow
For old, unhappy, far-off things,
  And battles long ago: 20
Or is it some more humble lay,
Familiar matter of today?
Some natural sorrow, loss, or pain,
That has been, and may be again?

Whate'er the theme, the maiden sang   25
  As if her song could have no ending;
I saw her singing at her work,
  And o'er the sickle bending;—
I listened, motionless and still;
And, as I mounted up the hill,   30
The music in my heart I bore,
Long after it was heard no more.
          —WILLIAM WORDSWORTH

The fact that this poem is not equally good in all of its parts does not mean that it is unadmirable. Perhaps no poem is perfect or could be; and perhaps an appearance of perfection is the most suspicious appearance a poem can put up. At any rate, here is a famous poem that deserves its fame, and yet each stanza is inferior to the one before it. The first, which is the best, has none before it, and in fact contains or expresses the whole of the impulse that was moving Wordsworth as he wrote. Not as he saw this Highland girl, for he never saw her. He read about her in a prose book of travels, Thomas Wilkinson's *Tour in Scotland*. Wilkinson saw the solitary lass, and wrote a sentence about her which made Wordsworth in effect see her too—made him, that is, see her as a poet. Many great poems have come thus out of books: most commonly, out of prose books. Prose discovers the matter and leaves it clear; after which the poet has only to write his poem as if the matter of it were his own, as indeed it comes to be.

Wordsworth is most deeply interested in the fact that this girl in his mind's eye inhabits a solitude. It is not the solitude of Pound, Whitman, or Peele. There are many solitudes, and the present one is Wordsworth's own of which he always wrote so well. He puts the reaper into it and makes her belong there, a figure undefined except by the fact that she stands alone in a world which has no content other than her thought and feeling. Her mood at the moment is melancholy in the sweet way that Wordsworth understood so well. Good and healthy persons, in harmony with their surroundings, are both sad and happy there. They do not comprehend their universe as it weighs upon them, but they love it and can therefore bear its weight—gravely, because it is so huge and old, but joyfully too because they feel their strength as they do so.

The first eight lines say all that Wordsworth really has to say about this, and about the girl who is his symbol. "Behold her, single in the field." She is single; she is solitary; she is by herself; she is alone—we are told four times, in five lines, that this is true, as if nothing else matters, and nothing does for Wordsworth. Also, she is singing. She is a peasant girl, and she is singing as her kind is disposed to do, sadly, sweetly, and powerfully to herself. The folk knows, if civilized men do not, how the weight of the world is borne by those whose turn has come to be alive in it. Such is Wordsworth's deepest conviction as in his imagination he watches the girl. The eight lines put her clearly before us, bending gracefully as she sings some song of which he says only that it is melancholy, and that it is loud enough to fill a whole valley.

> O listen! for the vale profound
> Is overflowing with the sound.

If these are the best lines in the poem, the reason is their mysterious power to create the thing they mention. The deep valley fills with music as we listen; and overflows. This is partly a matter of onomatopoeia in the lines themselves, and partly a matter of their rhythmical relation to the six lines above. The eight-line stanza Wordsworth has decided to use—perhaps he is deciding only now—consists of a quatrain and two couplets. To point this out is not to explain the force we feel in the series as Wordsworth manages it. Few poems have begun more happily, or so rapidly achieved so much momentum. The initial quatrain, tetrameter except for its short fourth line which so sensibly halts us for a scrutiny of the thing, the person to be seen—the girl herself, bending down and rising up, reaping and soliloquizing—is followed, once we have checked our progress and stopped to gaze, by two melodious pairs of lines whose rhymes flow into one another as if by magic, producing in us a lively sense of the music which takes its rise in the maiden, fills the valley around her, keeps on filling it, and overflows. The two couplets are in a sense one sound, drawn out indefinitely and continuing in our ears, so that the remainder of the poem, no matter what it may say, will be assured of an accompaniment, a ground harmony, a remembered song that hums in the mind long after its occasion has ceased.

Having done this much—and it was a great thing to do—Wordsworth henceforth is reduced to conscious reflection upon his subject. The reflections are fine and the poem as a whole is fine, but nothing in it, not even the second stanza, quite matches that opening section in which the subject was created—all at once created, by no effort that could be observed, and by no means that we may be altogether sure of naming rightly.

The first reflection takes the form of a comparison. The song we heard was beautiful and strong; there is no doubt of that; but Wordsworth must suspect us of doubt, or he would not tell us how much better it was than something else. Than the voice of the Arabian nightingale; or the voice of the cuckoo in spring, among the farthest Hebrides. South or north, he insists, there is nothing to compare; and yet the comparison proceeds. The fact that it is a double comparison does not help to justify it. The girl's song is said to be more exciting than either of two distant sounds; and we believe this, yet are left thinking of those distant sounds, which replace hers. The second of them in particular is rendered with genius. The two compound words in line 14, "spring-time" and "cuckoo-bird," reinforce each other so freshly that one of them seems to spring out of the other as a rocket springs out of itself, bounding off with redoubled speed and joy. In two strokes of its wings the line mounts high and flies away, taking us with it to remote and moveless seas which nevertheless tremble when this sound arrives. "Breaking" is the word. It creates the very silence it shatters, softly and far away.

The stanza is noble, yet less so than the one that rendered it unnecessary. And the rest of the poem goes steadily downhill. The third stanza is of all things a rhetorical question, or worse yet, a pair of them. "Will no one tell me what she sings?" Certainly no one will, for Wordsworth is the authority. He does not understand these Highland words, or the girl is too far away for them to be heard, but that is no matter. The net meaning of the song is his to know if anybody is to know it, and he should not be asking for assistance. Lines 18-20 are agreeably suggestive of a romantic burden which the words may bear; and as such they are preferable to the couplets (21-24) he dutifully writes because he remembers his own theory that great poetry comes out of familiar and domestic things as well as out of battles long ago; it is not a useful theory at the moment, but he jogs on through it, finishing the stanza at last. He has long since lost contact with his subject in its purity. The quatrain of this stanza was intrinsically better than its couplets; but it was in the quatrain that he strayed away, farther even than he had gone in the magnificent stanza about the sands of Arabia and the Hebridean seas.

The last stanza recovers a fragment of the magic that is gone, but only a fragment. "Whate'er the theme"—it begins prosaically, still reflecting upon a very unimportant topic. It moves then into a series of lines whose function is to fix in us a sense of the song's immortality. We had that sense at the end of the first stanza, and noted it then. There is no objection to our being reminded of it at the end of the poem—the poem, Wordsworth seems to be saying, will end but the song will not—and yet there is little chance that we shall be excited by learning something we already know. Wordsworth throws his discourse into the past tense—"I saw her," "I listened"—but this is a mere device of syntax. "I listened, motionless and still." That is better, for it suspends both him and us in a state of listening where it is possible to lose ourselves. This had been, however, our original state, which the second and third stanzas interrupted; and perhaps it is not available to us again. Indeed it is not, or to Wordsworth either, judging by the pious assurance he gives us in the last three lines that he will not forget an unforgettable experience. The experience, in fact, is dead; though we can always revive it by returning and rereading stanza one. That is the contribution of the poem, and it alone makes the entire work admirable.

13. Composed upon Westminster Bridge

September 3, 1802

Earth has not anything to show more fair:
Dull would he be of soul who could pass by
A sight so touching in its majesty:
This City now doth like a garment wear
The beauty of the morning; silent, bare,   5
Ships, towers, domes, theaters, and temples lie
Open unto the fields, and to the sky;
All bright and glittering in the smokeless air.
Never did sun more beautifully steep
In his first splendor valley, rock, or hill;   10
Ne'er saw I, never felt, a calm so deep!
The river glideth at his own sweet will:
Dear God! the very houses seem asleep;
And all that mighty heart is lying still!
                              —WILLIAM WORDSWORTH

In the smaller compass of a sonnet Wordsworth has arrived nearer perfection than he did in "The Solitary Reaper," though the sonnet is not better for this reason than the poem. It is good in its own right; nor should we conclude too hastily that perfection was more approachable in the shorter form. A sonnet can be bad, and many sonnets seem long. If this one moves powerfully and smoothly toward its end, and gives us its subject whole, in terms of the subject itself, the simplest explanation is that Wordsworth was a great poet, capable first of feeling and conceiving the essence of a subject, and then of finding words and rhythms competent to transmit that essence to us.

The subject is a city at sunrise. Wordsworth, passing through London on a stage coach in the early morning of the date he gives, saw it suddenly as a living thing about to wake from sleep—though it was still asleep—and composed his sonnet while the vision was still before him, probably without paper or pencil, in his head as was his custom. The remarkable thing for him was that the city seemed beautiful at this moment. He had been used to thinking and saying that only valleys, rocks, and hills (line 10) are ever beautiful in the pure, serene way of which he was now aware. He was and is the poet of natural solitude. Lakes, bald mountains, deep groves, and lonely cottages were for the most part the matter of his song. He had lived in London once, and had rejected it as ugly and untrue. Yet here it was, a great, calm, almost holy thing, a breathing creature with its eyes closed, as patient and wise as any landscape he had been worshipping in his northern retreat. So he put it down.

He started with a statement to prove (line 1), and went on dangerously (line 2) to accuse anyone who might disagree with it. To accuse him of dulness; and this is indeed dangerous, for it is a charge we instinctively resent and resist, particularly when brought by poets. Wordsworth had then to proceed at once with his proof, and to succeed with it if he could. It was the only proof of which poetry is capable—such a rendering of the subject as to make it seem, to all our senses and our intellect, the thing it was claimed to be. The city of London had to be made to look and sound like the thing Wordsworth himself was gazing at. Or merely to look, for there was no sound. The silence of London had been perhaps the first thing to strike him. All of it now is silent as we see it through the eyes of the poem; and there is power in the silence.

The third line is the real beginning. The majesty of London is "touching"—a rare word for the thing it modifies, and likely to fail unless well used. It is used well by being placed well, centrally in a simple line, and balancing in its *ch* the *j* of "majesty," so that the adjacence of rich sounds itself creates a sense of something important and self-sustained. Then comes the fourth line, which runs on into the fifth. It might not have done so, for this is an Italian sonnet, and the opening quatrain of such a sonnet is ordinarily closed. But Wordsworth's instinct is to increase his speed, and the run-on does it for him. We are drawn at once into a stream of lines that henceforth never pauses or stops. Scarcely have we had time to note that Wordsworth says the city wears *the beauty* of the morning, not the morning, when we encounter a series of words—two adjectives and five nouns—which pulls us into the center of the object and shows it to be crowded with detail. The ships, towers, domes, theaters, and temples pile high and wide for us to see. It is a veritable city, such as we ourselves have known, and the same sense is there of life that could strangle itself in its own excess.

Not that Wordsworth wants us to think this. So he tells us in the last two lines of his octave that all things here are at peace—

> Open unto the fields, and to the sky.

The pell-mell series ceases all at once and we hear, in a line full of quiet vowels, that the restless citadel is now at last not restless. It is as much aware of the ground and sky around it and above it as a mountain in the Lakes would be, or as a shepherd dozing by a rock. It exists out of time as ordinarily it knows time. It is a dream city,

> All bright and glittering in the smokeless air.

The absence of smoke, so casually mentioned in one passing word, not only explains the brightness of the dream but assures us of the sleep that would make it possible.

The sestet moves still more rapidly, through a rhyme scheme perfectly suited to this purpose. The last six lines of an Italian sonnet can be rhymed at will in any combination of three sounds. Wordsworth chose the combination *cdcdcd*. It is the most forthright of them all, the most imperious, the most persuasive. At least it seems so here, in his potent hands. The poem takes on new energy and races to its end like a happy animal certain of its goal.

> Never did sun more beautifully steep
> In his first splendor—

the trochaic "never," the long, rippling adverb before "steep," and the run-on into another line where a second series will be heard, work with the word order to suggest a fresh excitement in the beholder's mind, an excitement which the six rhymes, rushing like a waterfall, are all the while conveying.

Yet one of these six lines is independent of the rest. "The river glideth at his own sweet will"—the Thames, which Wordsworth had seemed to forget, asserts itself and commences flowing. It is the only thing in the picture that moves, and it moves at its own sweet will, without relation to the domes and temples. It was there before they were, and it never sleeps. It glideth now, as it ever does, on its winding way to the sea. Yet in a sense it does not move. A river is the one thing of which we can say that it both runs and sleeps; its water changes, but its form is constant. So the Thames, given thus its sudden, separate line in the sonnet about to close, seals as it were the silence of the city. Its peace is more powerful than that of the towers and theaters because it is the peace of sleep that is still not sleep. Motion and stillness at once—the Thames contributes this miracle, and makes the poem all that it could be. Of its own will, too, as if Wordsworth had nothing to do with the act. His only act was to put the river in the poem, in the best place and at the best time, with an air of irrelevance that should not deceive us.

14. The Garden

How vainly men themselves amaze,
To win the palm, the oak, or bays,
And their incessant labors see
Crowned from some single herb or tree
Whose short and narrow-vergèd shade   5
Does prudently their toils upbraid,
While all the flowers and trees do close
To weave the garlands of repose!

Fair Quiet, have I found thee here,
And Innocence, thy sister dear?   10
Mistaken long, I sought you then
In busy companies of men.
Your sacred plants, if here below,
Only among the plants will grow;
Society is all but rude   15
To this delicious solitude.

No white nor red was ever seen
So amorous as this lovely green.
Fond lovers, cruel as their flame,
Cut in these trees their mistress' name.   20
Little, alas! they know or heed,
How far these beauties hers exceed!
Fair trees! wheres'e'r your barks I wound,
No name shall but your own be found.

When we have run our passion's heat,   25
Love hither makes his best retreat.
The gods, that mortal beauty chase,
Still in a tree did end their race;
Apollo hunted Daphne so,
Only that she might laurel grow;   30
And Pan did after Syrinx speed,
Not as a nymph, but for a reed.

What wondrous life is this I lead!
Ripe apples drop about my head;
The luscious clusters of the vine   35
Upon my mouth do crush their wine;
The nectarine, and curious peach,
Into my hands themselves do reach;
Stumbling on melons, as I pass,
Ensnared with flowers, I fall on grass.   40

Meanwhile the mind, from pleasure less,
Withdraws into its happiness;—
The mind, that ocean where each kind
Does straight its own resemblance find;
Yet it creates, transcending these,   45
Far other worlds, and other seas,
Annihilating all that's made
To a green thought in a green shade.

Here at the fountain's sliding foot,
Or at some fruit-tree's mossy root,   50
Casting the body's vest aside,
My soul into the boughs does glide:
There, like a bird, it sits and sings,
Then whets and combs its silver wings,
And, till prepared for longer flight,   55
Waves in its plumes the various light.

Such was that happy garden-state,
While man there walked without a mate:
After a place so pure and sweet,
What other help could yet be meet!   60
But 'twas beyond a mortal's share
To wander solitary there:
Two paradises 'twere in one,
To live in paradise alone.

How well the skillful gardener drew   65
Of flowers, and herbs, this dial new;

> Where, from above, the milder sun
> Does through a fragrant zodiac run,
> And, as it works, the industrious bee
> Computes its time as well as we!　　　　　70
> How could such sweet and wholesome hours
> Be reckoned but with herbs and flowers?
> 　　　　　　　　—ANDREW MARVELL

Of this matchless poem there is a matchless part, the middle part, which all the rest envelops and protects. It contains what for Marvell is high and holy doctrine, and he saves for it the peculiar, the beautiful wit of which he is master. It consists of three stanzas among the total nine: the fifth, sixth, and seventh, which are themselves a poem within a poem, a shining masterpiece wrapped in poetry of a different order from its own—a lesser order, though the wrapping is beautiful too, and adapted with perfect cunning to its purpose. The first four and the last two stanzas are incomparably clever; the middle three are great. That is the difference, and Marvell intends it. A qualification would be that the middle three are clever too, and that the surrounding six are greater than most poetry is. To accept this qualification is only to mean once more that stanzas 5-7 are in a category by themselves. Cleverness in them has become genius, has broken through to truth; and it could not have done so unless it had been of a very high order from the beginning of the poem.

Marvell buries the heart of his work in a thicket of ingenuities which he hopes will entirely absorb and satisfy us if we are incapable of withstanding the full force of his secret doctrine when it comes, or if we are likely to smile at the miracles and paradoxes it promotes. He tosses us conceits and fancies which we shall be so busy playing with as not to notice when his voice changes, his vision deepens, and poetry (or as he would have said, wit) substitutes for what we think is sense.

The title is "The Garden," and the first four stanzas lead us to suppose that Marvell is engaged in nothing but extravagant praise of charming retreats where trees and flowers grow. How mistaken men are, he begins, to labor and perplex themselves in the pursuit of human honors, each one of which requires a single-minded devotion payable only in the limited coin of palm or laurel. The greater the effort, the meaner the reward; whereas if peace were sought, if repose were the good desired, all flowers and trees are ready to supply it—all of them as one closely woven, collaborating entity, a garden.

In his own garden, Marvell seems to be saying in the second stanza, he has found at last the quiet and innocence he formerly sought among men. These things were not there, and could not be there. They are sacred growths, they are supernatural pleasures, which here on earth will be found only where other growths are found—in gardens. He understands now that society at its finest is but barbarism compared with this delicious solitude where society is not needed; or where the one true society exists, of plants with one another and with any human mind prepared to know and love them in their own identity.

What society calls love, for instance, is nothing to this love. Poets by an old convention connect amorous thoughts with the colors white and red; but this green is lovelier. The world's lovers, strolling idly into any garden, wound its trees by cutting in them the names of their mistresses. They do not know how much more beautiful the trees are than the mistresses. If Marvell ever carves names in bark, they will be the names of the trees themselves.

When men are too old for love, they regularly retire into gardens. They are like the gods in that respect—the gods, for example, whom Ovid treated in his *Metamorphoses*. They were always changing people into other things—Daphne into a laurel, and Syrinx into a reed. Ovid thought this was done for love of the persons chased; but the truth is, Marvell now realizes, that Apollo pursuing Daphne, and Pan pursuing

Syrinx, had no other thought than to produce more vegetation, since vegetation was the thing they really loved.

So for four stanzas Marvell has proceeded, dazzling us with ideas which as he states them, in crisp octosyllabic couplets and with consummate craft, are delightful enough for common purposes. If he has suggested, or even actually said, that gardens have something of divinity in them, he has seemed to be exaggerating, as poetry is licensed to do. All but the best poetry, that is. For now the best poetry is coming, and though it will achieve even prettier craft than that in lines 15-16, we shall not be judging it by craft alone. And though it will take the subject into mystical recesses unguessed before, and altogether reproportion it in the divine dimension, we shall not accuse it of exaggeration. Things wonderful beyond our wildest thought will be stated as fact. We shall be, if we are reading well, where poetry transforms the world.

The fifth stanza of the poem, and the first of the hidden masterpiece, says: Now! the true, the ideal garden, the paradise of paradises, the reflection in time of all that is eternal, lies about me for enjoyment. At last it is safe to speak of it; and I shall begin by describing the pleasure which it gives my body. The children of the gods, of whom I now am one, live effortlessly, in a garden that feeds and refreshes them without their having even to be conscious of hunger and thirst. So with me at this moment. Ripe apples, luscious grapes, the nectarine, the curious (rare) peach, and melons underfoot—I am intoxicated by delicate plenty, I am dazed by generous ease, so that I wander unaware, am caught amidst a wealth of flowers, and fall, but fall without injury, on grass that is there to be my cool, soft couch till I get up again to stumble among the riches of this place.

But that is only my body; that is nothing but pleasure. At the same time my mind discovers happiness—a greater thing, and more mysterious to describe. The sixth stanza, the most famous of the nine, describes it. Not only is the mind a sphere wherein all things outside it are reflected and repeated (the brain of man contains the universe as in a nutshell); it is something more wonderful still. It creates new worlds that never were; or else it makes over in its own image, and in the image of what it loves, all things that were formerly made: annihilating them, as it were,

> To a green thought in a green shade.

The couplet which this line completes is as much more brilliant than the couplet at the end of the second stanza as it is more difficult to paraphrase. It defies paraphrase, partly because none is needed if the intoxication of stanza 5 has been convincing, and if lines 43-46 have done their work. In such a case the reader knows without being told in any other way than this how far he has left the world behind.

But there is still the soul, the last and greatest of man's three parts. The sixth stanza wisely searches for a little symbol, not an immense one, and finds it in a bird with silver wings that sits among the boughs, preening itself for flight. It has abandoned both the body and the mind to glide into the foliage where we watch it; it still, however, has a long way to go, for it will leave this world. It is the only part of man that can do so. Meanwhile, though, it sits and sings, and catches on its plumes the many-colored light which it will exchange at last for the pure white light that shines elsewhere than even here.

The masterpiece is done. The body, the mind, the soul have had their moment of being alive and visible, of being created in man's language. Now the poem can return to the surface where it originally disported itself; cleverness once more is in order. We get a full charge of it in stanza 8, where we hear Marvell's mind—not the mind of stanza 6, but the social mind that has ideas and writes verse—turning its wheels again. Adam's paradise, he remarks, must have been something like this. But only before Eve came. She did not multiply Adam's pleasure and happiness; she divided it in half. And indeed this was inevitable, since he was but a mortal man. Paradise as he had had it was too good for him. It was Paradise twice over, being his alone. He could not bear such happiness, and so was given the fraction of it proper for two inhabitants.

The final stanza brings us altogether out of the maze at whose center poetry had sat. The theme is time, which we had left but which we have again in the form of a sundial. It is a remarkable sundial, made of herbs and flowers, and bees compute the hours with its fragrant help. The poem, in other words, still dangles wonders before us. But we are free of it at last. And we are far from the center where the soul had made its own melody while the mind created worlds and the body swooned in sensual delights. It was a fabulous place, more real than bees and trees but harder if lost to find again. Poetry has never found it again as Marvell found it in three stanzas.

15. To Meadows

Ye have been fresh and green,
　　Ye have been filled with flowers;
And ye the walks have been
　　Where maids have spent their hours.

You have beheld how they　　　　　　　　5
　　With wicker arks did come
To kiss, and bear away
　　The richer cowslips home.

You've heard them sweetly sing,
　　And seen them in a round:　　　　　　　10
Each virgin, like a spring,
　　With honeysuckles crowned.

But now we see none here,
　　Whose silv'ry feet did tread,
And with dishevelled hair　　　　　　　　15
　　Adorned this smoother mead.

> Like unthrifts, having spent
>   Your stock and needy grown,
> You're left here to lament
>   Your poor estates, alone.   20
>   —Robert Herrick

The first two lines are fresh and green, and filled with flowers. This statement is a tautology, but there was no escaping that. The lines not only refer to something; they have it in them. "*Ye* have been . . . *Ye* have been"—the repeated opening is a vigorous dactyl, a phrase impetuous at the attack, and the "Ye" strikes a better first blow than "You" would have done. The alliteration of "fresh," "filled," and "flowers" helps also; as does the fact that no accent falls on "been"—the time is past, but for the moment we are not thinking of this. The flowers are alive and present, and fill the whole meadow as far as we can see.

Yet the third and fourth lines, slowing a bit the pace of the poem, make us look again and see maids walking—not now, for their time is already gone, but once at any rate, and perhaps not many days ago. It is almost possible to see them still, rhythmically crossing and recrossing the field of grass.

> And ye the walks have been
>   Where maids have spent their hours—

the movement is that of a light march, back and forth, this way and that, on lines that meet and separate. We can almost see the lines, the paths: a faint maze of tracings over the meadow.

The maids were silent so far as we yet know; or if they made sound, it was thin, light sound, as if they were imaginary girls. Is that not so, Herrick asks the meadow? And he is more personal now: he writes "You." They came with wicker baskets, walked to and fro, met one another in the paths, kissed as they passed, and stooped in rhythm to pick cowslips which they then bore home. Only the richer cowslips. For they were selective, they bent down only to the best specimens of the flower they sought; and "richer" goes well with "wicker," "kiss," and "cowslips" in this stanza. The music of the vowel is slight, as it should be: almost a whisper, as befits these noiseless, smiling creatures of another time. And "richer" is so much better than "richest" that Herrick is glad he was inspired to find it. It is a choicer word, and slips into the sentence exactly as those girls slipped into and out of the meadow.

They were not silent, however. They sang and danced—sweetly, in a circle, facing in. And each of them, doing this, was like a mythological figure of spring, slender and tall, and curved on a delicate stem, like flowers in wind. A crown of honeysuckle, if not actually on her head, seemed to be there, completing the effect of allegory. For these maids were both themselves and not themselves. If they were there at all, they meant more than they knew, as in older eyes, gazing from a distance, beautiful young things of any sort are bound to have a value of which they are unconscious. Flowers, girls, animals—it is true of them all. The difference in age, and the sense of passing time, enhances what is seen, as Herrick's thinking of these maids has already made them taller and more important, though they are still gentle, and their footsteps make little or no sound.

Yet even that changes as he watches and remembers. Herrick's fourth stanza, uniform with the others in the simplicity of its trimeter beat, still differs from each of them as each of them had differed from the others. The pronoun changes. He is not consulting the meadow any more; or he is including himself with it. Time has receded further, too—"now we see none here." The girls are gone; there is a real silence. It magnifies the sound they made when they were here—a real sound, and sometimes even a heavy one. Their silvery feet *did tread*. They beat the ground in the hard, fierce way of Maenads. The *d*'s tell us this, in two words coming after another one, and one before that, which had not prepared us for the surprise. Silvery feet can make no noise at all. These did tread, did tread. And the hair of the dancers was dishevelled, as in stanzas 2 and 3 it certainly was not. Another *d* in "dishevelled"; and still another one in "Adorned" (line 16), though "Adorned" assures us that the dancers still beautified the mead (a third *d*) they dominated. The mead was "smoother"—another comparative epithet, to match "richer" in line 8, but its function is not the same. For one thing, it is not quickly apparent what is smoother than what. Was the mead, when the girls did tread it, smoother than they? Or is it smoother now than it was then, and sadly so? Or is the reference to one part of the meadow that was then and still is smoother than any other part? Perhaps we do not need to decide, possessed as we are of a rich phrase, a good solid thing in itself.

The second meaning was probably the right one, stanza 5 suggests. Herrick addresses the meadow again, returning to the second person in order that he may charge it with negligence and unthrift. You had these girls, he says; you spent them; and now you are poor. So am I, but I was not the waster. They were your girls, not mine, and you let them go.

> You're left here to lament
> Your poor estates, alone.

The neutral vowel in "left" and "lament," and the alliteration of the words, lead us into the melancholy last line where we still hear an *l* but also hear the *o*'s of "poor" and "alone." Those girls who grew out of the meadow as we watched it have sunk back into its sod. All is quiet, all is brown, and winter is coming on.

Unless we can hear these things happening in Herrick's lyric we shall not know how dramatic it is. Lyric art, like any art, moves in the direction of drama—toward excitement, into it, and then away. The lyric means are often slight, and triumph instantaneous. But it is not trivial if we have good ears that can catch changes of meaning, sound, and movement. Herrick was so great a master of these that we can easily miss his greatness.

He called no attention to it, he simply had it, he simply did it.
He was a completely successful poet—the kind hardest to do
justice to, but the kind that best rewards the attempt.

16. The Flower

How fresh, O Lord, how sweet and clean
Are Thy returns! Even as the flowers in spring,
   To which, besides their own demean,
The late-past frosts tributes of pleasure bring.
         Grief melts away   5
         Like snow in May,
  As if there were no such cold thing.

Who would have thought my shriveled heart
Could have recovered greenness? It was gone
   Quite underground, as flowers depart   10
To see their mother-root when they have blown;
         Where they together
         All the hard weather,
  Dead to the world, keep house unknown.

These are Thy wonders, Lord of power,   15
Killing and quickening, bringing down to hell
   And up to heaven in an hour;
Making a chiming of a passing-bell.
         We say amiss
         This or that is;   20
  Thy word is all, if we could spell.

O that I once past changing were,
Fast in Thy paradise, where no flower can wither!
   Many a spring I shoot up fair,
Offering at heaven, growing and groaning thither;   25
         Nor doth my flower
         Want a spring shower,
  My sins and I joining together.

But while I grow in a straight line,
Still upwards bent, as if heaven were mine own,   30
   Thy anger comes, and I decline.
What frost to that? What pole is not the zone
      Where all things burn,
      When Thou dost turn,
And the least frown of Thine is shown?   35

And now in age I bud again:
After so many deaths I live and write;
   I once more smell the dew and rain,
And relish versing. O my only Light,
      It cannot be   40
      That I am he
On whom Thy tempests fell all night.

These are Thy wonders, Lord of love,
To make us see we are but flowers that glide;
   Which when we once can find and prove,   45
Thou hast a garden for us where to bide.
      Who would be more,
      Swelling through store,
Forfeit their paradise by their pride.
                —GEORGE HERBERT

Like Herrick's poem, Herbert's has to do with something
good that comes and goes, but instead of a single case it describes a series, the long series that is mortal life. Spring and
winter endlessly alternate, says Herbert, in the region of his
spirit. As flowers blossom and die, so he thrives and fails; year
after year the process is repeated, proving as it does so the
power of God who keeps it going. He wishes it could end, but
knows that while he is a man on earth it will not, any more
than it ends for the flowers. Now once more he revives and
feels the green of spring; also, he writes poetry again, and takes
delight in it. But this is only one more member of the series.
The goodness of God consists at last in intimating to him that

sometime it will cease. There is another garden—in heaven, not here—where he will neither bloom nor wither. It is paradise, which the greedy will never possess. It cannot be had here and now. It waits upon the time when time and change for us have died. It is something like Marvell's garden at the center of his maze; yet it is not that either. It is the Christian paradise. Herbert is a religious poet, and this is one of the great religious poems.

It is written in an intricate stanza such as Herbert loved to devise. The initial quatrain is inverted from the normal pattern which would make the first and third lines longer than the second and fourth. Here the second and fourth are the long ones; then come two very short ones—a couplet with only two quick feet in each line; and after that jerk or twist of the rhythm, a seventh line, matching in length the first and third, but rhyming with the second and fourth, closes the stanza at a slower pace. It is a stanza that calls for skill, to say the least; and Herbert had plenty of that—no poet more so. It also calls, however, for a rich subject in which there are many devious windings. Herbert's experience was such a subject, for it was the experience of God—to Herbert, both a simple and a mysterious Being of whom an infinite number of things were true. His task as he saw it was to entangle himself in these truths at the same time that he entangled himself in the net of a suitable stanza, and then to get clear if he could. The struggle was as good as the success, the pleasure of being lost as great as that of finding the way again.

Our pleasure is in the many triumphs tucked into the recesses of this verse; as when, for example, we hear the little couplet in stanza one leading us into that remarkable last line:

As if there were no such cold thing.

Eight monosyllables, and all of them accented; or at least the final four are accented. *No such cold thing*, we say; or rather the poem says it, insisting as it does so that we pay special heed to each familiar, natural word. *As if*—those two are important also, for there is really no *as if*. There *is* such a cold thing, and the poem will speak of it often enough. But already it has brought to life the wonderful willingness we have each spring to believe that nothing save spring exists. If we must conquer the illusion, that is another matter, and the seventh stanza will take care of it.

"My shriveled heart" (line 8) is "green" again (line 9). With this one statement Herbert brings into the same view himself and the flowers, which he wants us to think of together. My heart, the metaphor decides, and every other human heart as well, is a plant which God kills and quickens (line 16) in his power (line 15). From the hell of despair, of spiritual drought, it is no time at all, or at the most an hour (line 17), to what we think is heaven. It is as if the very bell that was tolling for someone's death had changed into a chime (line 18). But we only think our new state is heaven. It is not the true heaven, it is that imitation of it which comes in spring, or comes in the form of a momentary, seeming success. And it is subject to the terrible frown and wrath of God, who again in no time at all can alter things for the worse (stanzas 4-5). The growing had been at best a groaning (line 25), an immense expenditure of effort; and all for nothing. Ice turns to fire in a single instant (lines 32-35); the heart is shriveled again.

And now (stanza 6), though I am old and this thing has happened to me many times, it is happening once more. Rain has come to cure my mental death as inspiration has returned to my earthly art, my poetry.

> I once more smell the dew and rain,
> And relish versing.

The pleasure is great, and Herbert describes it with infectious glee; yet he knows now as he never knew before how little it means. The Lord of power has consented to appear as the Lord of love, and to make him see what this mad waking signifies. It is not rebirth, though it feels like that. It is the shadow of re-birth in the forest of this life. Elsewhere is a garden where he and we may be ourselves forever: not flowers, nor even men, but proper inhabitants of paradise.

The stanza makes the poem, given of course the feeling in Herbert that can fill it, and the understanding that works through it like a golden thread.

> It cannot be
> That I am he—

the nervous couplets, speaking so suddenly at the center, give the long lines much to do, and give us, the readers, a startled, full sense of the struggle going on. It goes on everywhere and all the time in this rich poem which an ancient child most earnestly is spelling out.

17. The Oven Bird

There is a singer everyone has heard,
Loud, a mid-summer and a mid-wood bird,
Who makes the solid tree trunks sound again.
He says that leaves are old and that for flowers
Mid-summer is to spring as one to ten.   5
He says the early petal-fall is past
When pear and cherry bloom went down in showers
On sunny days a moment overcast;
And comes that other fall we name the fall.
He says the highway dust is over all.   10
The bird would cease and be as other birds
But that he knows in singing not to sing.
The question that he frames in all but words
Is what to make of a diminished thing.
                                        —ROBERT FROST

Not everyone has heard the oven bird in midsummer, or known that he did. For any reader, then, the first line of this poem may be statistically untrue. But the rest of the poem makes it ideally true; we are given the bird, and given thoughts about it, so that it lives and speaks and has the authority it desires.

It speaks, not sings. "He says." Three times a line begins this way, and another line tells us that he knows indeed how not to sing when song would make no sense. The oven bird flourishes in that dry season which stretches between two other seasons: the early petal-fall of spring, when pear and cherry bloom go down, and the fall we *name* the fall, when all the leaves will drop and the summer die. Now is the very prime of summer, but it is not a singing time, since there is nothing to sing about. The trees hang in full leaf, gathering dust; they are not old enough to fall but they are old; and everywhere a peculiar silence is in charge, as if the summer slept out its richest days and did not want to be disturbed. The whole year is suspended in a state of health which it holds on to doggedly, day by day, as time prepares that other fall to come.

Meanwhile the birds have ceased, but not this bird. As we go by the deep woods we hear from their interior a loud voice— "teachér, teachér"—that strikes the very tree trunks into sound again. Those trunks had been somnolent, like the branches and leaves; they had stood there like dead things; but now they have an answering voice that repeats what the oven bird is saying. He says, as if to himself but loud and clear, that leaves are old and that there is no comparison between this time and the time of the spring flowers. He is even mathematical about it—the ratio is one to ten. He says the time will not return when blossoms showered like raindrops, on days of alternating sun and shadow. He seems to know and remember Shakespeare: "The uncertain glory of an April day." He says the other fall is coming but has not come. He says that dust for a long time has been drifting in from the highway, and settling everywhere, a film of white or grey on everything. Perhaps that is why he keeps on using his voice; some dust is in it now, but if it stopped altogether it would choke and fail. He will exercise it, dry as it is, and keep dead silence away. He will dare the dust with one repeated sentence, which if we listen long enough will say these things—and more, too, if we understood. He too would be silent but that he knows what to do now that song has become impossible. Something is diminished—the occasion for joy and song—and substantially what he is doing is putting a question: "What shall I make of the fact? How may one, in spite of dust and seeming death, keep speech alive?"

To paraphrase the poem thus is not at all to state its force, which we feel to be sure as something said, but said with so relevant a music that we scarcely recognize it for music. It is there nevertheless, and its composition is masterly. The poem is a bundle of lines, each one of them falling complete, each one of them resonant with surprise. The content is laid down, line by line, with firm and humorous distinction. The beginning startles us if we are among those who have never heard the oven bird. We probably have not; but in the second line we do—in the still more startling "Loud," and in the two words that match each other: "mid-summer," saying when, and "mid-wood," saying where. They say it confidently, cockily, as if someone, to seize our attention, had knocked on wood. Then, in lines 4 to 10, the message comes, in a dry, penetrating monotone that does not avoid the idiom local to this place. "For flowers"—the phrase can hardly be translated, yet we know what it means: "as far as flowers go," "with respect to the number of flowers in bloom," or something like that. Lines 6 to 8 are homesick for a beautiful, fresh time that has gone and will not come again this year. It was such a time as Herrick dealt with, but the suggestion is not that it has gone forever. There is merely this present waiting-period, which the bird's voice punctuates with two statements that have in one sense nothing to do with another.

> And comes that other fall we name the fall.
> He says the highway dust is over all.

The first statement is delivered so entirely in the idiom of speech that we search for the place where a certain accent should fall. The line is iambic pentameter, so there are five accents; but what about the last two? Did the bird, whose monotone continues, drowning all accent, say "*we* name the fall," "we *name* the fall," or "we name the *fall*"? Probably the second, but no one should insist. In any case the bird has been prophesying; and he returns at once to the present hour. "See?" he says. "The dust. It comes in from the highway—has been coming every day for weeks and months—and is over all." The rhyme is particularly telling here. All of the rhymes have been telling, for these pentameters chime in a strange, wayward fashion, promising a sonnet (the poem is fourteen lines) yet giving none. The rhyme now is expressive of the dreariness the bird suddenly feels, remembering the dust; though it is a dreariness he can overcome, for he keeps on talking. Or we assume so.

Actually, at this point the poet takes over and finishes the poem with his own quatrain—about the bird, not by him. Even the middle of the poem was in indirect discourse, with no expressed claim that the lines reproduced a text. Now the poet, in a voice singularly like that other one we have been hearing at remove, goes on.

> The bird would cease and be as other birds
> But that he knows in singing not to sing.

He is singing after all, yet we wouldn't call it song. "In singing not to sing"—that is highly musical, but it seems interested only in what it says. Frost, who wrote it, is a great lyric poet who tries to disguise the fact that he is, and does this so well that he has fooled people. He has merely wanted to make sure that his song made sense; was not idle music. Poetry is not literally music. It is only the music that spoken words can make —no more, no less.

Or it may indeed be true that our time is not a lyric time.

Many have said so. Very well, then. If the possibility of song has been diminished by some accident of history, and the twentieth century is not a singing age, what does a poet do? What does the oven bird do, annually in the forest from which music has retreated? He makes the solid tree trunks sound with something anyway. Everyone has heard him, including every poet. That is how it might be done. Not sing, but say. Not poetry, but conversation.

The only trouble is that the poem in which all this has been accomplished is witty, is rich, is real, is interesting, and is musical. Rhymes do not happen thus in toneless verse, nor do lyric ages produce anything better than the weave of this rhythm—each line laid into the whole with astonishing economy and grace. Poetry and humor are one in "The Oven Bird," as they are one in every singing century.

18.   Once by the Pacific

The shattered water made a misty din.
Great waves looked over others coming in,
And thought of doing something to the shore
That water never did to land before.
The clouds were low and hairy in the skies,   5
Like locks blown forward in the gleam of eyes.
You could not tell, and yet it looked as if
The shore was lucky in being backed by cliff,
The cliff in being backed by continent;
It looked as if a night of dark intent   10
Was coming, and not only a night, an age.
Someone had better be prepared for rage.
There would be more than ocean-water broken
Before God's last *Put out the Light* was spoken.
                    —ROBERT FROST

Change is coming in this poem; it has not been. Frost's oven bird looked backward toward a time of rain and petal-fall, and forward toward another fall that would finish everything; but only for a year, and meanwhile there was the question what to do with the quiet time between April and October. Here, however, there is the possibility of utter change, of dark times coming when wrath and might will be at war with all that is. There are defenses, as the continent has first its cliffs and then itself to oppose the hungry ocean, which like Shakespeare's ocean, in the sonnet that begins "When I have seen by Time's fell hand defaced," labors to "gain advantage on the kingdom of the shore." The speaker, standing by the Pacific as a storm drives waves against a world of rock, becomes aware of how much strength is in the drive; how much fury; and considers whether there is enough land, enough cliff, enough continent to endure. For the water will keep coming in, and the land had better be prepared for a siege. So had the people on it better be prepared for a crisis. Not for a night, but for an age. The waves as they reach the cliffs will break and be broken, but something else will too. Whatever it is, and we are not told what it is, premonition says it will be serious. The end of the world? If so, it will take a long time, and much will die in the process.

The seven couplets that accomplish this add up to as many lines as "The Oven Bird" contained, but there is no chance that we shall expect a sonnet. The couplets drive on as the ocean does, one after another, looking hard ahead—even over one another, as Frost says the great waves do. For each brings more with it than the previous one had brought; its burden stands higher on its back, and threatens more terrible things. There is no doubt of it: this is a poem of premonition, answering the fears men have today. The fears, or the exultations. The resolution in any case to say what worst future has been seen, and to be armed against it with whatever emotions are available. A sonnet might have said as much, but the couplets do it better. They strike seven notes on the gong of prophecy. "The Oven Bird," thinking its way through time gone by and present and to come, distributed its rhymes in a complexer pattern, be-fitting a complexer meditation. Here there is no meditation at all, unless we want to inflate the word. This is prophecy itself, which if it speaks does not do so in sonnets. It hammers at us seven times, then goes back into silence.

The voice is vernacular, as if no special person spoke. Any-one might be saying what is said here. "Thought of doing something"—the understatement is radical, and might even be absurd had not the first two lines created the ocean as they did. "You could not tell, and yet it looked as if"—the line sounds tentative, sounds timid, as if the speaker were out of his depth in an overwhelming subject. He even forgets the rule of gram-mar that would ask for "were" instead of "was" in lines 8 and 11. Or is "was" better? It is for him, and so he uses it; and makes it right. "Lucky," and "backed by"—the words are those a man might use who did not know we would overhear.

Yet he is a poet; that is to say, he is not limited when it comes to expressing a thing. He is not poetical, he never spoke this way before; but the *shattered* water makes a *misty din*—that is how it really is, and so he says it. The din is misty, and so is the sky above it—not far above it, for the clouds are low. They hang and blow like hair in front of sinister eyes. There is a kind of face behind all this, a purpose that gleams in the gathering dark. You can't tell, but it looks as if the dark were going to last. Not for a night, but for as much time as we know of as coming. An age, a new age. Such things do not come easily; we do not wake up and find ourselves in the next era. We go through wars to have it, and perhaps through centuries of rage, of real conflict which nobody enjoys.

The speaker then is both a person and a poet, both plain and powerful in his speech. His idiom is ordinary, but that does not prevent him from achieving enormous results with it, as here where the great waves coming in mount one upon another like beasts with a common purpose, and still another beast looks on from the low mist of sky above the water; or as where (lines 10-11) the simplest possible words put into act the whole of an imminent epoch. The wrench of the meter in the second of these lines opposes with peculiar force the two parallel terms, "a night," "an age." An age of darkness it promises to be, a long night and a terrible one.

The present time is full of premonitions, most of which are expressed at greater length than this. It took wit for Frost to be so brief. Wit in poetry is not so much an ingredient that graces it as the essence of the thing itself. The century of Donne, Herbert, Herrick, Carew, Lovelace, and Marvell knew the secret of this, and indeed its name for poetry was "wit." It knew better than any other century thus far has known how to say difficult things with ease and modesty. But the secret is not lost if Frost can say as much as he has said in fourteen lines. They seem easy and are serious; they entertain and shake us with the same familiar words. "You could not tell, and yet it looked as if . . . Someone had better be prepared." They almost prepare us, even; though not quite. Poetry does not save the world. It says what the world is—a hard thing to do, and rarely done.

19. The Second Coming

Turning and turning in the widening gyre
The falcon cannot hear the falconer;
Things fall apart; the center cannot hold;
Mere anarchy is loosed upon the world,
The blood-dimmed tide is loosed, and everywhere   5
The ceremony of innocence is drowned;
The best lack all conviction, while the worst
Are full of passionate intensity.

Surely some revelation is at hand;
Surely the Second Coming is at hand.   10
The Second Coming! Hardly are those words out
When a vast image out of *Spiritus Mundi*

Troubles my sight: somewhere in sands of the desert
A shape with lion body and the head of a man,
A gaze blank and pitiless as the sun,   15
Is moving its slow thighs, while all about it
Reel shadows of the indignant desert birds.
The darkness drops again; but now I know
That twenty centuries of stony sleep
Were vexed to nightmare by a rocking cradle,   20
And what rough beast, its hour come round at last,
Slouches towards Bethlehem to be born?
    —WILLIAM BUTLER YEATS

Change again, as in Frost's poem, is coming rather than has been. Yet that is not true either. Change has been—centuries ago—and is returning. The first revolution was the coming of Christ, and now a second one is due, or overdue. The world is in so bad a way that surely the Second Coming is at hand. The words speak themselves; and the poet, hearing them, has a vision. The darkness lifts long enough for him to see, far away on some sandy desert, a strange beast stir slowly, as out of endless sleep. The darkness drops again, but the vision will remain. It is clear now that some rough beast, this one or another, is on the move to where he will be reborn. This is the revelation. This will be the revolution.

The first of the two sections into which Yeats divides his poem names the symptoms of disorder in a world—our world —where change is overdue. Communication and authority have ceased. The falcon, soaring away from the falconer who should be able to call it back, has already spiralled so high, and the curve of his flight describes such distant circles, that the very pattern of the relation is lost in space. So is relation lost between all parts of the world. The center of gravity exerts no pull on things which once knew where that center was. The result is anarchy, that waited for this moment to flood a landscape once laid out in figures properly placed, or at any rate fixed in their positions. The flood has arrived, and it is not bright like water but dim with blood. The forms of life (line 6) are over-whelmed as the faith that kept them working, even though it did not understand them, itself is overwhelmed and drowned. What are the specific signs of this, the human signs? The best of living men do not know any longer what to believe, either with respect to the old forms that were or with respect to the new forms that ought to be if any are desired; or with respect to the nature of existence, the truth about the world. As for the worst men, the ones who once could be ignored, and even wished to be ignored, they are no longer quiet. They are the passionate ones, the intense ones who will have their way regardless of the horror this suggests.

Horror is the subject of the second section. "Surely . . . Surely"—the repetition of the word expresses an urgency not to be withstood; though only by degrees is the future defined. At first "some revelation," and only after that the thought of a parallel between this time and the time preceding Christ's appearance that so changed the world—when was it, twenty centuries ago? The accompanying vision troubles the poet's sight, which cannot interpret it as agreeable, however sanctioned it may be by Spiritus Mundi, the Spirit of the World. The beast that stirs has the body of a lion and the head of a man; and has a gaze, as it looks perhaps in this direction—though it is not important where it looks, and indeed it may be looking off—as blank and inhuman as that of the sun's disk when it burns for no reason except its own heat. We look at the sun but the sun does not look at us; or if it does, there is no feeling in its gaze, and certainly no pity. There is no discrimination at all. Meanwhile it is noticeable that the body of the beast moves a little—slowly, but there is no doubt that it moves. Any part could have been mentioned, but it is the thighs, the slow thighs, we see. They remind us of the lion body, crouched in sleep; and they are vast members, we somehow know, of a body which itself is vast, and buried perhaps a certain depth in the sand. It has been there a long time with-

out moving, so that the birds of the desert have become accus-
tomed to it as they would to a monument, a Sphinx. Is it the
famous Sphinx of Egypt? Not quite, for Egypt is the wrong
place, but the image will do. In any case the birds, aware of its
movement, reel indignantly above it, their shadows reeling
with them on the ground and in the air; the shadows, indeed,
are all we see of them, and soon even they will be invisible as
darkness drops again. The darkness does drop; the veil descends; and the poet is left with his knowledge

> That twenty centuries of stony sleep
> Were vexed to nightmare by a rocking cradle.

He knows, in other words, how serious and sinister the
change has been, will be. Are the twenty centuries those before the original Coming or those between that time and now?
The second answer suggests itself, since this is the twentieth
century after the birth of Christ. If so, the sleep of the mon-
ster has been unquiet all the while—vexed with nightmares of
the Nativity, the rocking cradle where the infant lay who
revolutionized man's and earth's existence. If the first answer
is right, however, we are to understand that for twenty centuries this beast foreknew in his dreams the change that would
come in what for us was the year one. It may not matter how
we decide, in view of the certainty that such a beast is there,
and that he is not Christ himself. He has nothing to do with
Christ, except in so far as he expresses the awfulness of change
on so huge a scale. Christ may have looked that way too to
those who feared him or lost by his coming. But that is not it
either. The beast is simply the beast of change—real change,
that waits and then upheaves the world. The present world
demands his waking—the first section of the poem is still true—
but the cure may be more terrible than the disease. Revolution
is not lightly to be asked for, or gaily to be prophesied. Revelation has its terrors as well as its beauties. In this case it is the
terrors we are moved to think about, somewhat as the beast

itself—a beast of stone, apparently, an ordinarily insentient be-ing—is moved to stir his thighs as he rouses himself out of the sleep he would prefer to prolong and goes towards Bethlehem to be born. Or, since it is a cycle that is closing, a curve that meets itself, an hour that comes again as come it must, he goes to be reborn. But it is a beast that goes. Not Christ, unless Christ was the beast two thousand years ago. If that was the name then, another name is preparing to be spoken now. What name? The poem does not know. "What rough beast—" the last thing is that question, unless it is the shaggy image of the slouching sphinx that goes to perform his pitiless function for at least the second time in history. Doubtless it is more than the second time, but we lack the knowledge that could count them all. More than human time, perhaps, is involved. The beast of change is no respecter of persons or times.

The twenty-two lines of blank verse which thus diagnose our world and predict the death that will precede its recovery are notable, as were the lines of "Once by the Pacific" and "The Oven Bird," for the naturalness with which they spell their statement out. They could be units of prose for all the air they have of being conscious that they are parts of a poem. They have no such air. Each line, each sentence says only what it must, and says it with the force of prose at its best—and prose at its best, as every poet knows, is a powerful thing. But this in fact is verse, and verse of the highest order. No two lines are alike, and no one line is artificial; but a principle of rhythm is working without rest to magnify the statement being made. Of the eleven syllables in line 15 the supernumerary one is of course in "pitiless," where the excess will be most effective—literally, most pitiless. Two accents fall together in the next line, on "slow" and "thighs." That is how we are made to feel the strength of what we see; it is a sluggish strength, but we know by this how inexorable will be its use once all the body is aroused. "Reel," at the beginning of line 17, deserves no accent and yet takes its full share, as is right in view of the activity it suddenly describes. This means that we shall pronounce hastily the words "of the," but that again is right since it gets us on immediately to the in*di*gnant *des*ert *birds*, who need the three heavy stresses they are given in consequence, matching at the other end of the line the two in *Reel shad*ows. In line 20 a cradle rocks; in line 21 "rough" dislocates the meter in order to have the importance in it we shall not doubt that it deserves; and how could the sense of line 6 be communicated in any other series of words than those we hear? They are courteous words, ceremonious words. The rhythm slows its progress in the key word "innocence," which we are led to speak with a full sense of what it means or once meant, and with pity in our voice because that quality is drowned. Mastery of verse is found only in master poets. It is the sign that they mean what they say, and that they know how to convince us of this.

20.   The Cat and the Moon

The cat went here and there
And the moon spun round like a top,
And the nearest kin of the moon,
The creeping cat, looked up.
Black Minnaloushe stared at the moon,   5
For wander and wail as he would,
The pure cold light in the sky
Troubled his animal blood.
Minnaloushe runs in the grass
Lifting his delicate feet.   10
Do you dance, Minnaloushe, do you dance?
When two close kindred meet
What better than call a dance?
Maybe the moon may learn,
Tired of that courtly fashion,   15
A new dance turn.

Minnaloushe creeps through the grass
From moonlit place to place,
The sacred moon overhead
Has taken a new phase.   20
Does Minnaloushe know that his pupils
Will pass from change to change,
And that from round to crescent,
From crescent to round they range?
Minnaloushe creeps through the grass   25
Alone, important and wise
And lifts to the changing moon
His changing eyes.

—WILLIAM BUTLER YEATS

A smaller beast moves in this poem than moved in "The
Second Coming," but he may not be less important. Certainly
he moves more: he creeps, he runs, he dances, and he creeps
again—indeed we are told three times that he creeps. He is a
black cat who seems to own the earth; no other creature is on
it, and there is but one thing visible in the universe above—the
pure cold moon, which Minnaloushe is constantly aware of
and would like to control as he controls the grass and shadows
among which he creeps. But perhaps he is controlled. The
sacred moon overhead may be more than he can manage. Does
it learn from him or he from it? The poem puts the question;
and meanwhile it creates a remarkable scene in which there
are but these two actors, so curiously interested in each other,
so different and yet so much alike. It is as if there were nothing in the world but moon and tide. Black Minnaloushe is as
much smaller than the tide as he is smaller than the vast man-
headed lion of "The Second Coming," his cousin by many re-
moves. But he is not less worthy of our attention—unless, to
be sure, we are persons who do not know how philosophical
a cat can be.

This cat is created to be seen and heard, and even to be
understood.

> And the nearest kin of the moon,
> The creeping cat, looked up.

All of his body—close to the ground, with neck stretched and eyes staring—exists in the second of these lines, as his habit of prowling and complaining about that incomprehensible thing in the sky is clear to us from "wander and wail as he would." Suddenly, however, he alters his behavior.

> Minnaloushe runs in the grass
> Lifting his delicate feet.
> Do you dance, Minnaloushe, do you dance?

We know by the springing verse that Minnaloushe has ceased to wander and wail. He is as serious as before, but now in silence he does the thing he can do so well—leap and trot, intending that his antics shall be seen. A cat is an actor, and puts on shows; this time, a show of running. Or is it of dancing? Is he trying to make the moon dance too? Its pure cold light had troubled his animal blood, and the fashion of its movement had been too courtly for his comprehension (line 15). If in fact it had "spun round like a top" (line 2), that was nothing to his taste. The spinning was done in place—a circle whirling on its center—and that was no motion at all. He should forget the moon and go about his earthly business. But he cannot forget it. It seems to be different from anything he is, and yet there is this strange attraction between them. Very well, then: a new dance turn. Do you dance, cold moon, do you dance?

It does not dance, and Minnaloushe, with a celerity peculiar to cats, gives up. Once more (line 17) he goes creeping through the grass, from one place to another where the moon's light falls, and refuses to look up. He will not be attracted or affected any longer. Yet he is, in spite of himself. Even as he creeps there, intent upon ignoring his faraway companion,

> The sacred moon overhead
> Has taken a new phase.

Even if he had been looking he would not have seen it. The moon's phases pass imperceptibly into one another; even the astronomer's eye does not see what his mind knows is happening between one mathematical moment and the next. Does the cat understand anything of this at all?

> Does Minnaloushe know that his pupils
> Will pass from change to change,
> And that from round to crescent,
> From crescent to round they range?

If we like we may hear in these lines the same old cat-voice wailing and complaining. Particularly in the last two, where the repeated "round," alliterating at the end with "range," reproduces the *miaow*, so plaintive and prolonged, with which any cat says clearly that something is not as it should be. But the lines are doing a more important thing than that. They are asking a strange question. Does Minnaloushe know what we know, namely that the pupils of his eyes have phases even as the moon does? Is that the similarity between them, the family resemblance? The pupils of a cat's eyes, to be sure, do not literally range from crescent to round, from round to crescent. They are a circle or a line, or they are any ellipse between. Only if seen from the side would they go through the moon's evolution; and even then the range would be from a semi-circle to a vertical line, not from a circle to an arc.

Yeats may be having the same trouble with the moon in this poem that Donne had with the sun in "A Lecture upon the Shadow." But what of that? The question is still startling, and still legitimate. The moon is there and the cat is here, and phases are in both. The question again is, does the cat know? The poem leaves him in an attitude from which we can learn as much or as little as we like.

> Minnaloushe creeps through the grass
> Alone, important and wise
> And lifts to the changing moon
> His changing eyes.

He is creeping and looking up at the moon as he did in the fourth line long ago. But now he is important and wise, and of course alone. Has he understood, and does he present his changing eyes to be admired and approved by the equally changing moon? Or does he move in his original ignorance, and are his importance and wisdom the qualities he would take with him in any case? Is he alone merely among the objects of earth, or is he alone with respect to the moon too, which he still stares at as at something alien and cold, the one thing he cannot master? At any rate *we* know. Or do we? The question is all we have as we go on watching.

The trimeter lines, so many of which carry an excess of syllables in deference to the nimble beast that moves among them, are rhymed in quatrains, yet the affinity of sound is sometimes as doubtful as the knowledge Minnaloushe has of his kinship with the moon. "Top" and "up," "would" and "blood," "place" and "phase" miss each other by a margin comparable with that in the cat mind, creeping and looking up. Trimeter, meanwhile, is proper for the poem as a whole, and it is never abandoned or obscured. It can go as slowly as it pleases—witness lines 4, 8, 14-16, and 25-28. Or it can leap and skip, as most of the time it does. It is as much lighter and rapider than the pentameter of "The Second Coming" as the subject of the one poem is freer than that of the other. Change is the subject of both; but here we have it as an endless, dancing thing like light on waves—the shimmer of a world that always changes yet is still itself. In "The Second Coming" it was seen closer up, as it affects men. So seen, it can be terrible, as waves look high to those they may destroy. Seen farther off, as the moon sees the ocean or as a philosopher sees both, they merely seem to call dance turns. The difference between Yeats's two poems is one of the signs by which we may know his range as an artist, and the range of poetry itself.

21. Brahma

If the red slayer think he slays,
   Or if the slain think he is slain,
They know not well the subtle ways
   I keep, and pass, and turn again.

Far or forgot to me is near;   5
   Shadow and sunlight are the same;
The vanished gods to me appear;
   And one to me are shame and fame.

They reckon ill who leave me out;
   When me they fly, I am the wings;   10
I am the doubter and the doubt,
   And I the hymn the Brahmin sings.

The strong gods pine for my abode,
   And pine in vain the sacred Seven;
But thou, meek lover of the good!   15
   Find me, and turn thy back on heaven.
          —RALPH WALDO EMERSON

The principle of change that looked so different from the two points of view established in Yeats's poems disappears in Emerson's poem altogether. It is an Oriental poem, inspired by Emerson's reading in the Sacred Books of the East, and in harmony with that alien source it denies both difference and change. All is one; there is no many. Or the many is an illusion, like the contraries men imagine to exist. There is no here, no there, no then, no now; nothing happens in a universe where change cannot take place; nothing happens, and nothing is—nothing, that is, except the mind that expresses itself in these sixteen mysterious lines.

    The lines are calm and regular; their voice is soft but decisive. The quatrains have the neat power of an engine whose wheels turn almost noiselessly, one within or behind another. The rhymes are not loud, but again they are decisive: they give the poem an effect of motion, though by logic there can be no motion. They help to turn the wheels, as the contraries keep them balanced in revolution. The contraries are denied, but their very mention is like a hand upon the spoke.

If a man thinks he acts, this is only because he believes there is such a thing as action. The red-handed murderer thinks he has ended a life; and the murdered one thinks he does not live; but neither of them knows the silent, subtle truth, which is that I exist. Action does not exist, but I do; and the motion I seem to make is only the whirring of wheels in place. I keep, and pass, and turn again—that is, I look as if I went away, but what men see is my returning. I have never left, in fact. Life neither ends nor begins, except in those who are born and die. The principle of life, beyond deeds and individuals, is stationary; it is myself, who always am. I am not here, I am not there. I am.

The first stanza says this, and says more with the help of its rhythm; or rather, it says it better. The two adjacent stresses in line 2, on "slain" and "think," slow the movement and even stop it for a second; then off the poem runs again, all the more rapidly in lines 3 and 4 because of the check it had been given by our having been forced to read:

> Or if the *slain think* he is slain.

More rapidly, and more pleased.

> They know not well the subtle ways
> I keep, and pass, and turn again.

It is almost mincing, it likes itself so well.

The second and third stanzas dispose of seven contraries—not quite one to a line, but close enough to that for the effect of miracle. Near and far, dark and light, absent and present, evil and good, end and means, thinker and thought, singer and song—of each pair both members are myself. And again the rhythm reinforces the content, giving it indeed a terrible charm such as our list of terms would never exert. The rhymes, as it were, advance the analysis and make it seem exhaustive; "same" and "fame" have even a third one, "shame," buried in its line to suggest confusion of riches.

If line 10 is especially triumphant:

> When me they fly, I am the wings;

its triumph is still heard in the firm accents of lines 11 and 12. "I am the doubter and the doubt" is the loudest line in the poem, and the next one is the proudest. The two definite articles, placed where they are, conspire with the humming monotone of syllables 4, 7, and 8 to suggest that the song of the Brahmin, beautiful as it may be, is nothing compared with the fact that I, unknown to the Brahmin, am its singer—am the song itself, which a priest with half-shut eyes believes he causes.

The fourth stanza is inferior to the rest in so far as Emerson lets it descend into homily. In a poem which denies the difference between evil and good, or shame and fame, there is scarcely a place for exhortation. The speaker should not care what we do or do not understand. The truth is what it is, necessarily, and does not need to state itself. Until the last two lines it might have been assumed that the singer had only himself for audience, as the wind does, or gravity, or a circle as it draws itself in space. In lines 13-14 he had reached the peak of self-congratulation: he had said that even the gods, the sacred Seven, envied him his power, his simple being, and were as ignorant of its secret principle as men are, or worms, or stones. But now he stoops to give commands, and to a nameless individual at that. Leave off thinking of good as you have hitherto imagined it, he says; it is not meekness, as you thought; there is no heaven in which it shall be rewarded; there is only me. Find me, and you will have it all. But this is scarcely possible, human understanding being what it is; and the final lines confess it by the comparative weakness of their words, their motion, and their rhymes.

Nevertheless the poem comes as near perfection as a poem can afford to come. The one flaw in it may be the thing that proves its power; or better yet, proves the power of him who speaks. While he speaks of himself, his true subject, he has an authority that cannot be doubted. This is all that matters in a poem whose author is searching for the very accent of authority. That Emerson found it, three of his quatrains and half of another one are evidence beyond question.

22. To the Memory of Mr. Oldham

Farewell, too little, and too lately known,
Whom I began to think and call my own:
For sure our souls were near allied, and thine
Cast in the same poetic mold with mine.
One common note on either lyre did strike,   5
And knaves and fools we both abhorr'd alike.
To the same goal did both our studies drive;
The last set out the soonest did arrive.
Thus Nisus fell upon the slippery place,
Whilst his young friend perform'd and won the race.   10
O early ripe! to thy abundant store
What could advancing age have added more?
It might (what nature never gives the young)
Have taught the numbers of thy native tongue.
But satire needs not those, and wit will shine   15
Thro' the harsh cadence of a rugged line:
A noble error, and but seldom made,
When poets are by too much force betray'd.
Thy generous fruits, tho' gather'd ere their prime,
Still shew'd a quickness; and maturing time   20
But mellows what we write to the dull sweets of rhyme.

Once more, hail and farewell; farewell, thou young,
But ah too short, Marcellus of our tongue;
Thy brows with ivy and with laurels bound;
But fate and gloomy night encompass thee around.   25
                                        —JOHN DRYDEN

The greatest change, for men if not for Brahma, is the change from life to death. Brahma has nothing to say about it, or nothing that we can understand; we have much to say, and we try hard to say it, though the subject is as far beyond our comprehension as the words of the god. Many poems are about death, and most of these have dealt with the deaths of individuals. Nothing new is ever said about the subject itself, but since individuals differ there is always something fresh to say about one life that was lived. Dryden's poem is addressed to a younger poet than himself who has died and taken his gifts with him. The poem is about those gifts; about the difference between them and Dryden's own; about the discrepancy in their ages; and about the older poet's affection for the younger, who is bidden farewell in the Roman manner, in heroic couplets which for Dryden were the nearest possible approach to Virgil's august and melancholy measure.

It is a literary poem, with a literary subject. Its protestations of grief are less interesting to us, and were meant to be less interesting, than its reflections upon the art of verse. Not that the feeling is insincere; but it is the feeling of one artist who regrets the disappearance of another, and thinks so well of the work he had done that he speaks chiefly of it. He is moved as he thinks of it to compare it with his own; to find a strong resemblance; to find one important difference; and to deny the importance of this difference after all, since it had seemed to be in his favor. In such a poem—it was written, in fact, to be printed as a complimentary preface to Oldham's collected work—everything said should be in favor of the person celebrated. Dryden magnanimously gives Oldham first place in his admiration as well as his affection. This is one of the noblest English elegies, and one of the most intelligent.

The alliteration and balance in the opening line—"too *little* and too *lately*"—would prepare us, if we were not already familiar with the form of Dryden's verse, for a serious poem which yet would bear in it many marks of the author's wit. Dryden had a mind and enjoyed using it; and he expected us to enjoy ours as we read him. He is saying here, with a formal flourish, that he wishes he had known John Oldham sooner and better; for now that Oldham is dead he has just begun to realize, and indeed to proclaim, that he was his own kind of poet (line 2). The two were much alike, the second couplet goes on to say; Oldham's verse made similar music (line 5), and both of them were satirists (line 6), with the traditional hatred of satirists for evil and stupid men. But the fourth couplet adds that though the two aimed at the same end, the younger man had reached it first; and the fifth brings in an illustration from the *Aeneid*. Nisus and Euryalus were two Trojans who participated in the funeral games for Anchises, Aeneas's father. The game in this case was a foot race, which the boy Euryalus won by taking over from Nisus when the old man slipped and fell.

Lines 11 to 22 are concerned with a question of art which Dryden now raises and settles. You were so proficient, he says to Oldham, at so early an age—what would you have gained by living longer? Or perhaps the question really is: What have we lost by losing you? There is one thing you had not perfected (13-14), namely the art of writing smooth and perfect verse—an art, incidentally, that youth in the nature of things knows nothing about, or at any rate too little. But for the purposes of satire this is unimportant; and in any case the kind of wit that is proper to satire can make itself felt even through harsh and rugged lines such as you wrote (15-16). That was to your credit, whatever your age; it is seldom that any poet, old or young, has more strength than his style can stand up under;

most poets have too little force of any kind (17-18). The triplet that follows (19-21) finishes the thought. Your work, though it ended too soon, was always alive; this is the main thing, and the most we can suppose is that with more years at your command you would merely have mellowed it, smoothed it, sweetened it, with the relatively dull and secondary merits which are all too common in the verse of poets who live long.

Once more farewell, the poem now concludes (22-25). You were young when you died, like Marcellus whom Augustus is said to have wept for when Virgil read aloud certain lines of the *Aeneid;* and like Marcellus you died too soon—blasting the same hopes for English poetry that the young Roman blasted for the future of the Empire. You are crowned with ivy and laurel now, in the underworld where Virgil himself is; but the night of that world is gloomy and perpetual, and I must leave you in it, the victim of fate which no man may resist.

The poem, then, says a number of things; and since it is a good poem it says them in fewer words than paraphrase requires. It says them with melody as well as wit. The heroic couplet is capable of much melody, and Dryden is its master in that respect, as indeed he is one of the best musicians in English verse. The pleasure of reading this poem is in large part the pleasure of hearing the sound it makes and feeling the rhythm it commands.

The first two lines, for instance, are very different in their movement; and the same difference appears between the third and the fourth, so that a kind of quatrain emerges, though it is not strictly that. The second and fourth lines, as distinguished from the first and third, run without interruption—of punctuation or caesura—to the end. There is no lingering over any syllable such as "near" in line 3; and the fourth line is particularly fast, as if the casting referred to were done all at once, in a mold ready-made for the performance. The six rhymes from "thine" to "arrive" are all on the same vowel—a high, clear vowel such as lyres might strike if their music desired to be successful. The sound is repeated at the beginning of line 11, in "ripe," but soon abandoned for the heavier note of "store" and "more," introduced with the thought of advancing age. The quadruple alliteration on the letter *n* in lines 13-14, and the neatness that makes line 14 so notable in general—by what better means could Dryden have suggested the quality he was concerned with? He quickly returns, however, to the long *i* we had heard above; for Oldham's lyre is playing again in lines 15-16, and we must hear once more that strong, high note. We hear it through three words that seem to make it difficult: "harsh," "cadence," and "rugged."

This is the best line of the poem, and indeed it is too good to be explained. "Harsh cadence" is a mysteriously effective pair of words, as "rugged" is surely the best epithet that could have been used in its place. But that is not all of it, nor can all of it be stated. The entire line runs to its end as the first and third did, with a speed and power that alone suggests the indomitable energy of Oldham's muse. The obstacles are there, but the line forces its way through them—not around them— with greater result because of their solidity. The singing voice breaks for a moment in the word "harsh," but recovers itself in "cadence" and is quite clear by the time we hear the rhyme word overcoming "rugged."

The triplet below, with its leisurely Alexandrine at the close, is perfectly employed. "Still (always) showed a quickness" is somehow an accelerated and accelerating phrase. Instantly, however, "maturing time" slows us down again, and prepares us for the dotage of line 21. Not only the presence of six feet does this; there is also the delay over "dull sweets," forced by the position of the definite article before "dull." By right of meter "the" deserves an accent, but the sense throws it forward to "dull sweets," where it drowses a long time before the poem resumes its march.

The Alexandrine that ends the poem is by no means so interesting; it is merely good enough for a closing flourish. And indeed the same thing can be said for the last four lines as a unit. They bring to its finish a magnificent piece of formal verse.

Such verse went long since out of fashion, but the fashion is worth knowing. The men who understood it—and none understood it better than Dryden—valued the virtues of firmness, intelligence, audibility, and harmony. There will never be a time when poetry can afford to be indifferent to those virtues. They exist in any good poem, and it is impossible for them to be there by accident. They must be honored consciously or not at all. They are not the only virtues in poetry, but when they are absent they are sorely missed. Where they are present, great verse is almost certain to be found.

23.   Drummer Hodge

They throw in Drummer Hodge, to rest
  Uncoffined—just as found:
His landmark is a kopje-crest
  That breaks the veldt around;
And foreign constellations west   5
  Each night above his mound.

Young Hodge the Drummer never knew—
  Fresh from his Wessex home—
The meaning of the broad Karoo,
  The Bush, the dusty loam,   10
And why uprose to nightly view
  Strange stars amid the gloam.

Yet portion of that unknown plain
  Will Hodge for ever be;

His homely Northern breast and brain   15
  Grow to some Southern tree,
And strange-eyed constellations reign
  His stars eternally.

                —THOMAS HARDY

Young Drummer Hodge, a casualty of the Boer War, is buried in this poem and dedicated to a hemisphere he had never expected to see. Least of all had he expected to lie down in it and sleep forever, under different stars from those he had known in Hardy's county of Wessex. Hodge is a common rural name, and its owner in this case is an all but anonymous boy, selected as later generations have selected the Unknown Soldier to stand for many more like him of whom there is nothing to say except that they died in action and were never properly interred or celebrated. Hodge has no coffin; he is thrown in "just as found," and the only object that marks the place is the top of a small hill nearby; it breaks the monotony of the open African country which otherwise stretches on and on in every direction, and indeed it is a mark by which any other thing in the neighborhood would be known. The invisible Hodge and the visible crest—that is all there is in this world except the stars at night, which are "foreign" stars whose constellations bear them westward over Hodge's mound.

The young drummer, who had come directly here from his English home, and who perhaps was never anywhere else on earth, had lacked the time—supposing he had the education—to take in the meaning of the new landscape of which as a soldier he was a part. He knew nothing of the vast plateau of South Africa, called the Karoo, over which he marched with his drum; he had never seen anything like the Bush in which the troops sometimes took cover, or the dry soil which was so different from his English sod. And when he looked up at night he had been unable to understand why the stars grouped themselves in these unfamiliar patterns. He was not an astronomer.

Yet he will always be a part of the plain where he lies. It was unknown to him, though he walked on it awhile; it is unknown even to us, in the sense that there is no record of his being there; or if there is, the precise place is not named in the record; and the record will disappear anyway. He will be a part of it in the same way that any bit of its earth is; his body —his undistinguished Northern breast and brain—will feed the roots of some Southern tree of which he never learned the shape; and those same strange constellations, looking down, will be his stars forever, as if he had been born under them instead of under Orion and the Great Bear, Hercules and Hydra and the Seven Sisters. He may never have called them by such names, but those were the ones he had seen each night in the Wessex sky. Now he will be watched by these, through an eternity of nights that except for the war would have been passed at home, under Corona and the Scorpion.

There could scarcely be a greater difference than the one between this elegy and Dryden's. Dryden's presupposed in its readers a willingness to remain within the classical, the entirely literary field of reference. It was a poem about poetry, and its English author left England only to pay homage to a Roman poet who was currently deified by the critics of London. Hardy opens to view a larger, barer, and more pathetic world. Not only is the veldt a place where no men are, and of course no poets; even the part of England from which Hodge came is barren of any learning other than that of peasants who do not know they are learned. Hardy's theme is ultimate in its simplicity. And so the poem is stripped of every suggestion that would defeat the effect desired.

Not that it was written without art. The signs of conscious care, once we begin to look for them, are almost as numerous as the words that are used. The stanza, for one thing, repeats itself with an apparent monotony, an almost mechanical insistence upon its form, which fits the regular mention of stars passing overhead—passing regularly, of course, since nothing is more ordered in its movement than the host of constellations. The unusual verb "west" at the end of the fifth line is all the more striking because of its position in the rhyme scheme. The scheme is the simplest possible: in each stanza the lines rhyme alternately, three times, and do so with acute emphasis, so that the pattern is never missed. In this case "west" is the third sound of its kind, and the emphasis is very hard. The foreign constellations *west* each night above the mound—the movement is what it must be and it will never change, any more than a failure of rhyme would have been tolerable here.

Each stanza has three pairs of rhymes, and there are three stanzas—not a coincidence of number by any means. The progress within any given stanza is the progress of the poem as a whole. For there is progress: the stanzas are not identical. Their differences are as interesting as their resemblances, though we are not intended to discover them so easily. The tense, for example, is always different. The opening stanza buries Hodge *now*. We see him thrown in; we look off at the kopje-crest that will be his landmark; we glance up and realize that after sunset there will be strange stars; but the moment is *now*, for all our thought about the future. That thought is not completed yet, though soon it will be—after a middle stanza which tells us where Hodge came from and how bewildered he was while he still lived and breathed this atmosphere. He was homesick, doubtless; but in any case it is the past tense in which we find ourselves, it is the origin and previous experience of Hodge that we are given. He is not a mere particle of human dust: he came from somewhere—the poet's own home—and he was mystified by the place he came to. Yet he died there; and the third stanza starts the process by which he will come to be identified with no other place. The development is rapid, as it must be in so short a poem, yet it seems deliberate too; and this last phase of it is not prophesied with unconcern.

The fifteenth line, probably the best of them all, is deeply charged with concern, not only in "homely" and "Northern," two rich adjectives which we shall be slow in pronouncing, but in the alliteration of "breast" and "brain," two terms so much better than "heart" and "head" (which also would alliterate) that it is impossible to measure the difference. "Breast" and "brain" are absolutely physical and absolutely affectionate. Far from being brutal in their plainness, the words assure us of Hardy's closeness to his subject—so close is he indeed that he touches it, pityingly, in these words that insist upon searching out the exact location of Hodge's body, which soon will be untouchable because undistinguishable from the dust and clay around it. Already, however, it is taking on the vitality it will have henceforth. It is preparing to grow into a tree—a strange tree, and for the third time we hear of strange lights in the sky. At the end of the first stanza they had been constellations; at the end of the second they had been stars; now they are both, and their eyes are exchanged for Hodge's. Once he had looked at them and wondered; they will look at him forever without wonder, accepting him as a part of a world that for them is neither old nor new.

Much, then, has happened between the first and last words of "Drummer Hodge." The three stanzas were alike and yet they differed. They had to, for all time was in their charge. All time, and all the still earth, North and South.

24. Praise for an Urn

In Memoriam: Ernest Nelson

It was a kind and northern face
That mingled in such exile guise
The everlasting eyes of Pierrot
And, of Gargantua, the laughter.

His thoughts, delivered to me   5
From the white coverlet and pillow,

I see now, were inheritances—
Delicate riders of the storm.

The slant moon on the slanting hill
Once moved us toward presentiments   10
Of what the dead keep, living still,
And such assessments of the soul

As, perched in the crematory lobby,
The insistent clock commented on,
Touching as well upon our praise   15
Of glories proper to the time.

Still, having in mind gold hair,
I cannot see that broken brow
And miss the dry sound of bees
Stretching across a lucid space.   20

Scatter these well-meant idioms
Into the smoky spring that fills
The suburbs, where they will be lost.
They are no trophies of the sun.

                                   —HART CRANE

There is precision in this poem, mingled with imprecision.
Somewhat as the face of Ernest Nelson, who now is dead, was
both northern and Latin in its quality, so the quality of Crane's
verse ranges from rigor to laxity. If the laxity is studied, and
so an aspect of the rigor, that again is like the thought Crane
gives to his friend. He both knows and does not know what to
think about "what the dead keep, living still." The poem deals
with that question, and preserves it as a question, suspending it
finally in the smoky spring that fills the suburbs, where with
every other question it will drift unanswered. Crane knows
how real the question is, and employs rigor to keep it real; but
at the same time he lets his lines wander with it as it leaves him
on its own unstated errand into regions of the ineffable. His

verses, like his well-meant idioms, respond to what he actually thinks as he writes; and when he decides that he does not know what to think, the poem reflects that situation too. It is a modern poem in that its content is complicated almost beyond the reach of words, but also in its unremitting effort, once this is granted, to make its words do all they can do.

The commas in line 4 lend to the first stanza an analytical air. The movement of the unrhymed quatrain (the whole poem will be unrhymed, though afterwards we shall have to look back and make sure of this) is deliberate and slow. "Kind and northern" is slow to say, and so is "exile guise," with its two accents driven hard together, and its two long *i*'s separated by an *l*. If the third line picks up speed, the commas in the fourth at once reduce it; they ask us to consider again the strangeness of the fact that this man with the northern face and name had yet the eyes of Pierrot—simultaneously merry and sad, and as old as the world of pantomime in France—and the gigantic laughter of Rabelais. But Crane does not say "the laughter of Gargantua." He reverses the word-order of the preceding line and says, like a scientist or a schoolmaster:

And, of Gargantua, the laughter.

The rest of the poem keeps firmly to its structure, but its author will never again know this clearly what he has to say. The second stanza seems to hesitate between a four-beat and a three-beat line. Each of its lines can be read as trimeter, and indeed the first of them can scarcely be anything else—His *thoughts*, de*liv*ered to *me*—but tetrameter is never far away, and soon enough, in line 9, it returns and establishes itself as the meter that will carry us to the end. Even this second stanza, however, has its firmness, its clarity of purpose. The nervous quickness of its lines matches Crane's uncertainty as to what Nelson had meant as he lay dying in bed. We are not told what the thoughts were that he "delivered"; only that they were "delicate riders" of some storm. What storm? Of time and oblivion? Of the history that stretches between the ancient culture that created Pierrot and the modern civilization in which some portion of Nelson lived as exiles live?

The third stanza, with its opening line that cannot be forgotten by anyone who has encountered it in its place, ignores the question and resumes the tempo of stanza one. Nelson and I, Crane seems to be remembering, once were moved by a strange junction of waning moon and sloping hill to consider whether we had not some presentiments after all of what survival means. The dead may keep something and live on. The soul has its properties which can be known, named, and assessed —again a formal, abstract term, reminding us of the commas in line 4 and "delivered" in line 5, not to speak of the precision every statement seems to be trying for.

Yet the claims of immortality, even then, are tentatively presented, as if the author himself did not know what to make of them. They are at once demolished by the crematory clock in stanza 4. The commas in line 13 are something like those in line 4, except that they have the additional function of suspending our attention while the clock prepares to tick, or strike, or whatever that clock did on the day when Crane, waiting in the crematory while his friend's body was burned, suddenly heard it. Perched on its shelf, apparently irrelevant to all things else, the instrument nevertheless "commented." And went on commenting, insistently. What was the comment? We are not told, though we can suppose that the mechanics of time had somehow replaced its metaphysics. Time? This is all there is to it, the clock may be assumed to have said; and as for *your* time—the era I am ticking off now—this is all there is to that, too, no matter how eloquently you and your friend once congratulated yourselves on living in it (lines 15-16). Time is nothing but a series of ticks, insistently the clock said, perched in the crematory lobby. The first line of the stanza, with its shocking intrusion not only of a crematory, and a crematory *lobby* at that (the very sound of the words is a brutal blow, breaking the poem at this point to bits), but of a machine on one of its shelves, is one of the most dramatic lines ever written into a lyric poem. And it seems to convince Crane that he has nothing further to say about the assessments of the soul. Pierrot, Gargantua, the history of human culture, and presentiments of immortality suggested by a classic moon—all this is swept away, along with generalizations about our time or any time.

Still, however, there is something. The gold hair above that northern face cannot be forgotten (line 17), nor can the beauty of that brow broken by suffering and imminent death. Death arrived, and nothing is left of Ernest Nelson to be sure —except, oddly enough, "the dry sound of bees." The fifth stanza is wonderingly, uninterruptedly slow. I cannot miss, says Crane, though I almost can, a curious sound of something going back and forth in spite of the emptiness that is there. It may not be human, but it is alive—a mere hum, a buzz, as if bees traveled the vacuum in question, and made it lucid after all. The statement is made, as has been said, wonderingly, and even incredulously. The three words at the end of line 17 all seem to be accented, though the first and third are the only ones that can be; and "dry sound" in line 19 takes as long to pronounce as Crane, saying it aloud to himself, requires to understand it.

But the net result is so uncertain that Crane decides to let the subject melt into thin air. It does so in the anticlimax of stanza 6, which is as skilful as any other stanza of this poem but naturally less vivid, since its aim is to leave our imagination nothing to work with. Let these words go, it says, these "well-meant idioms," and disperse themselves in the formless air that hangs over suburbs, where nothing is ever decisively known or felt. Even while spoken they threatened to scatter apart, having no cohesion in their speaker's understanding. They were never words of light (line 24). At best they were well meant, but that is only to suggest clichés—idioms everyone commands. Let them go, and let the poem fall apart. It is a modern poem, and bound therefore to begin more confidently than it can end. Modern art of any sort delights in frustrating its own form. It surprises by not surprising—by ending too soon, on a low note in a lower key. It is no triumph of the sun.

25. The Roman Road

The Roman Road runs straight and bare
As the pale parting-line in hair
Across the heath. And thoughtful men
Contrast its days of Now and Then,
And delve, and measure, and compare;   5

Visioning on the vacant air
Helmed legionaries, who proudly rear
The Eagle, as they pace again
          The Roman Road.

But no tall brass-helmed legionnaire   10
Haunts it for me. Uprises there
A mother's form upon my ken,
Guiding my infant steps, as when
We walked that ancient thoroughfare,
          The Roman Road.   15
               —THOMAS HARDY

The Roman Road runs straight and bare. Not only is that the first statement made by this poem, and its first line; it is the sense of the whole, from which no word, no rhythm, no image, no idea departs. Across the modern England Hardy knows, with all of its growths that more than twenty centuries have put there, growths of civilization and of vegetation, of institutions and of flowers and grass, an ancient thoroughfare, built once by conquering engineers, still keeps itself visible, as if the country's original skeleton insisted upon being

seen. Or, more specifically, its skull; for the second line contributes a remarkable image—the road runs as straight and bare
as the line across the top of a human head where the hair is
parted, showing the scalp beneath. Few images in poetry have
been more startling than that, or more successful—that is to
say, few images so bold have seemed so natural after all, once
they were understood.

If to any reader the picture is of a man's head bent down
in study so that the pale parting-line of his hair assumes an importance of which even he is unaware, with the result that no
thought he may be having interests the onlooker nearly as
much as the line does, so straight and bare across the summit of
his body, then such a reader is prepared for the three lines that
follow in the poem. There are thoughtful men—antiquarians,
professional or amateur—who busy themselves with the history
of Britain during and since its occupation by the Romans.
They talk about the differences between England as it is now
and as it was then; also, they make archaeological diggings,
take measurements, and compare their various findings. Some
of them, more imaginative than the rest, actually see the
Romans who once marched along this road. The vacant air
is peopled with a vision: legionaries with helmets, proudly
bearing the Imperial ensign, the Eagle, pace again the Roman
Road. Their progress is straight, along a line the poem has been
keeping straight—not only by the image of the hair but by the
forthright regularity of the rhythm, which in lines 4 and 5 was
even a dogged regularity, as if nothing could stop it, or stop
the men who delved and measured and compared.

Now in the second section (lines 6-9) a note of pomp is
added: the legionaries are proud under their helmets, and they
march confidently across a land they are convinced belongs
to them. They bear aloft a piece of Rome itself, the Eagle that
has flown here; and if there is any question about the straightness of the line they follow, Hardy has settled it by dropping
down in the space of the poem three words that lie there like

a ruler, levelling and keeping order among the host of syllables thus far heard. "The Roman Road." It is almost an overheard command, clearly capable of dominating even such powerful men as the movement of lines 6 and 7 has created.

> *Visioning* on the *vacant* air
> *Helmed legion*aries, who *proudly rear*

The stresses are radical and laborious—effortful, like the world conquerors who still fascinate a population long free of them.

"The Roman Road" lies again like a straight-edge under section 3, at the bottom of the poem. And this in spite of the fact that something entirely new has appeared in the section—something intimate and soft, something personal to a living man, something that has nothing whatever to do with Roman time. The living man is the author himself, who now tells us that the road means a different and special thing to him. He sees no men in helmets there—or no one man, for the image is singular, as befits the image with which it shall be contrasted. He sees his own mother, walking long ago on this same road, guiding his infant steps. The two of them, walking as one, make perhaps a frail image, decorated by nothing so grand as plumes or brass; but it is the only image he has, and he leaves it with us; but not before he has made sure once again that we understand how straight and bare the road both was and is. "Guiding my infant steps"—the four words alone have made this certain, although two others, "as when," hanging at the end of that same line until the next line should resume its march and tell the mother and child to keep on going, have done so too, as have three more, "that ancient thoroughfare," which required precise pronunciation if they were to be clear at all. Then at the end, dropped into place:

The Roman Road.

Why has Hardy worked for straightness in this fashion? Roman roads *are* straight—that is a fact, and good poems are true to facts. But there was another reason. He wanted to compare two kinds of time, and in order to do so he drew two lines in space—parallel and straight, to make comparison possible. One line is two thousand years long, and represents what history knows. The other line is, say, six decades long, and represents what one man remembers. And the shorter line somehow becomes the longer. That was Hardy's purpose, to be achieved by any means at his disposal. Some of the means he used have been mentioned, but not all of them, it must be admitted, can be known. All we are sure of is that the day when two small people trudged along this road seems farther back in time than the day when legionaries graced it with their plumes. For the legionaries are in a sense unreal, as history even at its best is bound to be; they are a reconstruction by the intellect of persons who indubitably lived and moved, but whom we cannot believe in the same way that we believe our own memories. Hardy's memory, which becomes ours, returns him to a moment that no amount of study could reconstruct, for there are no documents. It is all in his head, with its pale parting-line of hair. His mother's head is in its grave, but he remembers that ancient day, now remote in the mist of unrecoverable decades, when the two of them walked—probably west—along this road. Why mist is there we cannot precisely say; but it is there, and forms uprise from it to do the work they have to do. "Uprises," "form," and "ken"—such words assist them, surely, but they were there first, and remain.

26.   The Little Black Boy

My mother bore me in the southern wild,
And I am black, but O! my soul is white;
White as an angel is the English child,
But I am black, as if bereaved of light.

My mother taught me underneath a tree,   5
And, sitting down before the heat of day,
She took me in her lap and kissèd me,
And, pointing to the east, began to say:

"Look on the rising sun,—there God does live,
And gives His light, and gives His heat away;   10
And flowers and trees and beasts and men receive
Comfort in morning, joy in the noonday.

"And we are put on earth a little space,
That we may learn to bear the beams of love;
And these black bodies and this sunburnt face   15
Is but a cloud, and like a shady grove.

"For when our souls have learned the heat to bear,
The cloud will vanish; we shall hear His voice,
Saying: 'Come out from the grove, my love and care,
And round my golden tent like lambs rejoice.' "   20

Thus did my mother say, and kissèd me;
And thus I say to little English boy.
When I from black and he from white cloud free,
And round the tent of God like lambs we joy,

I'll shade him from the heat, till he can bear   25
To lean in joy upon our Father's knee;
And then I'll stand and stroke his silver hair,
And be like him, and he will then love me.

—WILLIAM BLAKE

It is difficult to imagine a poem that would sound more
childlike than this. It would also be difficult to find one that
was more complicated and profound. Blake's little black boy,
as if he were speaking a piece, delivers with effortless delight
an idea such as Dante would have loved and did indeed manip-
ulate in certain cantos of his *Divine Comedy*. The child keeps

going a singsong stanza of his own invention, seldom varying
the rhythm he takes for granted as perfect for his purpose.
Only in lines 11 and 12 does he take advantage of the infinite
variety offered by iambic pentameter to anyone who chooses
to play with the possibilities. And those lines are truly remarkable, not only for the series named in the first but even more
for the reversed beat of the second—trochaic or dactylic,
according as one's ear decides, but certainly not iambic.

> *Comfort* in *morning*, *joy* in the *noonday*.

The accents leap at the reader, certifying the comfort and joy
the sense of the words asserts. The series in line 11:

> And *flowers* and *trees* and *beasts* and *men*

is emphatic to the limit of emphasis, and suggests a thousand
other items in addition to the four there is room to list. The
monosyllables force themselves upon our attention as monosyllables do in every line of the poem. Seven lines are entirely
monosyllabic—fewer than we suppose when the poem is done,
for the effect has been constant. The child, looking steadily
at us, has spoken as if there were no long words in the language.
These at any rate would do for him, and to each of them he has
given its full value, as if everything depended on his speaking
the piece right. But we have no suspicion that it is not his piece.
He knows very well what he is saying. Child though he is, he
is master of an idea. His voice is the voice of authority, as that
of any philosopher is who has completed his thought. Really
completed it, so that he can put it into words of one syllable.

The boy's idea is everywhere in the poem, but it is most
directly stated in two monosyllabic lines (14 and 17) containing
the word "bear." The little black boy's mother told him one
hot day, as they sat in the shade of a southern tree, that the
souls of men endure with difficulty the beams of their Father's
love, which like the beams of the sun can burn and destroy as
well as nourish with everlasting life. God's love, beating fiercely

on a soul unprepared to sustain it, would bestow neither the comfort nor the joy that flowers and trees and beasts and men receive at noonday from the risen sun. Even then the bodies of men search out shadowy places, and benefit by clouds; for the heat of the sun itself is hard to bear. As nevertheless we learn to bear it, so in a parallel fashion our souls learn to bear the heat of love, which if we were exposed to it all at once would be as fearsome a thing as Dante found it in his *Paradiso*, where stage by stage he was disciplined to endure it and its accompanying light.

The parallel is not perfectly drawn, any more than Donne's parable of the sun, or Yeats's of the moon, could be pushed to its ultimate detail. Ideas are not finally physical, and phenomena cannot prove them. But this does not disqualify the attempt, which in Blake's case yields more than simple proof. For his real interest is not so much in the parallel as in the fact that there are black people and white people, and in his desire to persuade us that they are equals under the skin. The skin of either is but a cloud—in the one case black, in the other case white—which protects the wearer until the day when no pro-tection shall be needed; then both, having cast off their clouds, their skins, will be able to go where God is. The idea produces more complications, once Blake has translated it into terms of sun and shade, than the poem can take care of. The poem does not lose by this, but that is because Blake never lets us linger over the difficulties.

The boy begins by saying that he was born under the south-ern sun and therefore is black; but his soul is white—as white as the body of an English child, who because of his exterior is not misunderstood as black children are. I look, says the boy (line 4), as if I had no light at all, as if I had no soul; but my soul is inside of me as the soul of the English child is inside of him, and mine is as white as his. My mother explained this to me once, and made me understand a certain advantage there is in being outwardly black. She took me on her lap, kissed me, and pointed to the east where the sun rises. There God lives, she said, and sends forth His light and heat, and all things enjoy them. But we could not enjoy them as we do if we were not protected from their full strength. God for the time being has given us a cloud to cover us; it is like the shade of a grove; it is our color, which we shall continue to need until He decides that we have learned how to bear His love direct. Then He will call us out of our grove and we shall play like lambs around His golden tent. My mother told me this, the black boy says (line 21), and kissed me again.

And now I say to the little English boy, who does not know what I know, that he wears his own protective cloud—white, rather than black, but it is certainly a cloud. He has not learned this yet; he is deceived by its whiteness, which he identifies with the soul's whiteness. But there is no connection, any more than there is a connection between my white soul and my black body. The English boy doubts that I have a soul; he does not love me. But when our two souls are free of their respective clouds, and we stand around God's golden tent of which my mother spoke, I will shade him a little longer, until he has made up for his lack of discipline under the sun. Then we shall be equal lovers and friends, and I shall stroke his white hair; there will be no difference between us, and he will love me as even now I love him.

What are the difficulties we face if we insist upon under-standing all this literally and logically? In the mother's tale is God the sun—no more, no less? And if He is nothing but the sun, is it merely our distance from Him on earth that accustoms us to His beams? Supposing this to be so, how shall we be prepared for the sudden change when that distance disappears? And what heat will the English boy still feel in heaven—unless we have been right in assuming what the poem does not say, namely that the English boy has benefited from his white cloud less than he would have benefited from a black one? And is this a matter of his not having understood that there *was* a cloud? But a cloud is a cloud, and protects us whether or not we know it does. Also, does the northern child keep his silver hair—which has no connection with his soul—at the knees of God? And has the black boy the same complexion there? Is that why the two souls will love each other? Or are their bodies to survive, and the black boy's to become like the white boy's?

There are even more questions our paraphrase might arouse. For it is from the paraphrase, not the poem, that perplexities emerge. The poem itself is always simple, like the voice of the child who speaks it; and like his soul that speaks through it. For he has a conviction with which we cannot argue, since it is born of the very love that is his subject. His love of the English boy is more important than any proof he is advancing of their equality. Equality cannot be defended; it can only be felt, and the little black boy knows everything about how it feels. It is what reduces his sentences to the utmost simplicity—as when in line 22 he leaves out "the" before "little," and as when in the next line he omits any form of the verb *to be* after the pronouns. Above all it is what makes the last two lines so inexplicably moving. The stroke of a hand smooths every syllable and leaves it pure of everything except its own innocent intention; and the monosyllables in the closing line—like those in the seventh line of Herbert's "The Flower"—are invincible to any unbeliever. To anyone, that is, who before he read the poem had not known how equality feels. He still might have arguments against it, but he could not use them here. They would have no more effect on the little black boy's faith than the little black boy's argument, in so far as he has one, needs to have on anybody. The real poem, the poem we hear as we read, has left the body of argument as far behind it as the souls of the twin boys will leave their flesh when they become twin lambs that rejoice. It is all, of course, for the benefit of "little English boy," who had not known till now how much love was waiting for him in the southern wild.

27.

I. No longer mourn for me when I am dead

No longer mourn for me when I am dead
Than you shall hear the surly sullen bell
Give warning to the world that I am fled
From this vile world, with vilest worms to dwell:
Nay, if you read this line, remember not   5
The hand that writ it; for I love you so
That I in your sweet thoughts would be forgot
If thinking on me then should make you woe.
O, if, I say, you look upon this verse
When I perhaps compounded am with clay,   10
Do not so much as my poor name rehearse,
But let your love even with my life decay,
Lest the wise world should look into your moan
And mock you with me after I am gone.

—WILLIAM SHAKESPEARE

II. When I have seen by Time's fell hand defaced

When I have seen by Time's fell hand defaced
The rich proud cost of outworn buried age;
When sometime lofty towers I see down-razed
And brass eternal slave to mortal rage;
When I have seen the hungry ocean gain   5
Advantage on the kingdom of the shore,
And the firm soil win of the watery main,
Increasing store with loss and loss with store;
When I have seen such interchange of state,
Or state itself confounded to decay;   10
Ruin hath taught me thus to ruminate,
That Time will come and take my love away.
This thought is as a death, which cannot choose
But weep to have that which it fears to lose.

—WILLIAM SHAKESPEARE

[handwritten margin notes: "alternating rhyme = alternating of waves." ; "trochaic substitution" ; "important because shows complete meter reversal in thought as well"]

116 ·

These two sonnets by the greatest of poets are both love poems, but they are not alike. The first is perfect, and the second is great. The first confines itself to the relation of love between the poet and the person addressed; the second, assuming this relation, goes on to find a further subject—the largest one there is, for it is the whole world and all of time. "The world" is mentioned three times in the first sonnet, but the reference is not to the great world that includes every other action or object. Rather it is to the little world which lovers despise because it does not comprehend their love; at least this is true for "the wise world" of line 13. The epithet is ironic, and the implication is that people generally will be as heartless and indifferent as ever once the beloved is known to be bereaved. The "world" of lines 3 and 4 is a more considerable affair, yet the view is not substantially broader or deeper. It is the poor world we are familiar with in that convention of love which dismisses whatever is ignorant of the unique feeling lovers have. The world of the second sonnet is all the world there is, and it is an even greater thing than "my love" (line 12) which it contains. It is the subject all great poetry finally has, and certainly all great love poetry. The ultimate distinction of love is that it introduces us to reality; it is said to make the world go round, and that is doubtless true, but first it makes the world exist. Shakespeare in his second sonnet is as much in love as he is in the first, but the experience has taken him farther as a poet. It has helped him to discover the universe.

Not that the first sonnet has any least flaw in its composition. Few works of art have been more perfect. But it is the kind of perfection sentiment achieves. The lines produce a minor music that sings secretly to itself. Their burden of meaning is "I love you," and their art consists in finding not a larger but a lesser way to say this thing that all lovers have said since the beginning of romance. It is a tremendous thing to say, but poetry limits itself when it searches for nothing but minor variations upon a major theme. The lover in the present case may be supposed to have put the statement hitherto in every form but this, and now he tries this. Even it will fail, but it will have been one further attempt. How much do I love you? I will tell you again: If I should die before you do, I want you to forget me instantly—I sacrifice my dearest possession, your thought of me, to your continuing happiness, which would be diminished by grief and therefore must be free of grief, even though this means that you will forget my very name, and means that if you read this poem you will read it as if it were by some stranger. Also, I would not have you pitied by a world that sees how much you miss me. You must not miss me; you must let your love end with my life.

The music is absent from the paraphrase, and the music is the thing. It is sweet music, that loves its own melancholy voice, and encourages self-pity in the singer. Alliteration links word with word and line with line so that the tone is never broken; the sonnet is single to its close, is one uninterrupted sigh or moan that nothing ever prevents from luxuriating in its own existence. The long *o*'s, the *l*'s, and the *m*'s and *n*'s keep the poem liquid and sonorous, as the monosyllables do when used thus by a master. The monosyllables are his sign of an absolute sincerity, productive of an absolute simplicity, in somewhat the same way that alliteration certifies the fidelity of his feeling. The phrasing is intelligent and articulate—each small word does its work, and does it with economy—and that too is a sign that he means what he says. There is no question of this, or of the faultless pace of the poem as it moves toward its conclusion. Its only defect, paradoxically, *is* its perfection, its oneness and roundness. For the suggestion is of a subject that needed nothing but art to make it manifest. Here is art such as no other poet has, and it is wonderful in itself; but we might be happier still if we could catch the same poet in the toils of a subject that tested him to the limit.

He is so caught in the second sonnet, whose music is a double music, counterpointing the themes of life and love; or, if one prefers, of death and love. The three quatrains which according to Shakespeare's practice in the sonnet form make up the bulk of the poem all start with the word "When." With immense energy the overarching subject of the sonnet—not love, but Time—is thrice attacked. "*When* I have seen," "*When* I have seen," "*When* I have seen"—the march is a forced one, into territory hostile to "my love." It is the territory of Time's ravages: against masonry, against metal, and against the very shores of the world—but there a mutual devouring goes on, for the soil as often wins as loses, thrusting back the hungry ocean which in other battles conquers cliffs and beaches. *When* I have seen such things—and they are truly terrible things, suggestive of a force that nothing living can withstand—

> *Ruin* hath taught me thus to *rumi*nate,
> That Time will come and take my love away.

The drama of the sonnet, the resolution of the counterpoint, is in these two adjacent lines, the first of which raises to its climax the major music we have heard, while the second introduces, for one brief moment remaining, the minor music of the poet's personal love. The difference is in the power. Time itself is raging in lines 1 to 11; it is demolishing walls, it is corroding brass, and throughout the second quatrain it is rhythmically setting sea and land against each other. Lines 5 and 6 bring in the waves as Frost's poem brought in the Pacific: something not to be resisted. But line 7 checks the onslaught—quietly, in the third, fourth, and fifth words, all three of which, equally accented, back one another up like three columns of cliff rock —and line 8 communicates the sense of a mutual, never-ending give and take of alternately successful forces. The words thus far have been strong words, full of consonants and radically alliterating—witness "fell" and "defaced," "towers" and "eter-

JOHN MILTON

nal," "win" and "watery." Now in line 11 comes the weightiest alliteration of all; and then, with no warning, the utter disappearance of drums and storms out of the poem. Instead we hear the lonely voice of one man, high and thin, saying plaintively

> That Time will come and take my love away.

The big music is killed. Nothing can come after this but the muted couplet which leaves us with the lover as he contemplates his plight and almost regrets the love that was its cause.

It is a love poem still, but the subject has lost its narrowness. The speaker in the first sonnet, for all his sincerity, cannot escape the monotone that limits most of the love poetry in any language. The second speaker, who is no less sincere, finds himself nevertheless in a new dimension of the subject. Or rather, of the world that holds the subject in its place. We hear it there, holding the subject down, as two styles fight with one another. The drama of this great lyric is in the difference between its voices. It is not one thing, but two things that nevertheless are one in the glorious end.

28.

I. On the Late Massacre in Piedmont

Avenge, O Lord, thy slaughtered saints, whose bones
Lie scattered on the Alpine mountains cold;
Even them who kept thy truth so pure of old,
When all our fathers worshipped stocks and stones,
Forget not: in thy book record their groans   5
Who were thy sheep, and in their ancient fold
Slain by the bloody Piedmontese, that rolled
Mother with infant down the rocks. Their moans
The vales redoubled to the hills, and they
To heaven. Their martyred blood and ashes sow   10

· 120 ·

O'er all the Italian fields, where still doth sway
The triple Tyrant; that from these may grow
A hundredfold, who, having learnt thy way,
Early may fly the Babylonian woe.   14

—JOHN MILTON

II. To Mr. Lawrence

Lawrence, of virtuous father virtuous son,
Now that the fields are dank, and ways are mire,
Where shall we sometimes meet, and by the fire
Help waste a sullen day, what may be won
From the hard season gaining? Time will run   5
On smoother, till Favonius reinspire
The frozen earth, and clothe in fresh attire
The lily and rose, that neither sowed nor spun.
What neat repast shall feast us, light and choice,
Of Attic taste, with wine, whence we may rise   10
To hear the lute well touched, or artful voice
Warble immortal notes and Tuscan air?
He who of those delights can judge, and spare
To interpose them oft, is not unwise.

—JOHN MILTON

The difference between Milton's two sonnets—both of them in the Italian form—is a multiple affair. Were it completely stated, it would be seen to involve subject, diction, rhythm, tone, and indeed everything that operates when a poet creates and maintains a style harmonious with his theme. Milton knew all there is to know about that art, and we may take pleasure in following him into as many of its recesses as he leaves visible.

Both sonnets were written during the bitter and laborious years when politics took most of his time and strength. The first of them was written in wrath—in pity, too, and grief, but over all in wrath. His century was among other things a century of religious wars; he of course was not only a Protestant but a Puritan; and when news arrived in England, where he was an official in Oliver Cromwell's government, of a massacre on the Continent, he knew which side his sympathies were on. Certainly they were against the party that had perpetrated the massacre; and certainly this is clear from the sonnet the occasion forced out of him. It is one long groan of anger; it is a poem that leaves nothing unsaid or unsuggested, it assaults and blasts its subject, and while doing so it never takes a breath.

The octave runs on into the sestet—"moans," at the end of line 8, completes the first division of the sonnet but the sonnet does not pause. Ordinarily the sestet would then have offered us fresh rhyme-sounds; but here, in this extraordinary work, the long *o* sound that had been heard throughout the octave is carried on into at least three lines out of the ending six. Eleven of the total number have it; and it is the right sound for Milton's purpose, just as it is right that a majority of his fourteen lines should be run-on lines. Nine of them are, and in seven cases the rhyme-word that is left hanging is a long-*o* word; so suspended, it demands from our throats that moment's prolongation of it which a word well placed at the end of any run-on line demands. "Bones" (line 1) delays us between the powerful words "slaughtered" and "scattered," which in themselves produce an effect of rhyme although they have not that function. "Groans" and "fold" are simply suspended in their places; they draw out longer and longer the terrible tale Milton is telling. If we are still more radically checked in the pace of our reading by the late caesura in line 7, and by our curiosity as to what will come after the two words that follow the comma, surely this in the interest of our seeing and hearing what happens in line 8. "Mother with infant down the rocks" —the first three words send mother and infant down, and the next three dash them to their death. Again there is a late caesura; the punctuation this time is a period; and then we hear "Their moans," which the ensuing line echoes from valley to mountain, and which line 9, after a similar caesura, prepares for the heaven of line 10. "Grow" (line 12) is immediately reinforced by "hundredfold" in line 13, and both are abundantly answered by the two closing words of the poem, whose sense reminds us of the woe to be visited upon Babylon according to the Book of Revelation, but whose sound reminds us of the woe that every preceding word of Milton has embodied. The word becomes the thing, and we shall remember both as Milton in his indignation desired that we should.

All this is not to say that the sonnet chokes itself with undefined undifferentiated noises having only a general resemblance to one another. It is a highly articulate poem, as wrath can be articulate on intelligent tongues. It raps out certain of its phrases as if some object were being struck, or as if the lips of the chanter were snapping upon each other in their rage. "Kept thy truth," "stocks and stones," "Forget not," "The triple Tyrant," "learnt thy way," and "Early may fly"—each of these phrases is as crisp and distinct as the prevailing music is deeply mouthed; Milton's rage is alternately hot and cold, and the sign of coldness is this precision in the syllables, each one of which pronounces itself as if it were falling like a lash on the enemy's head and shoulders. But then the entire poem has its precision, in the sense at any rate that the chosen words, and the places chosen for them, never fail to do the work Milton set out to do.

The sonnet to his friend Lawrence, on the other hand, is light and choice in every segment of every line. The adjectives are Milton's, and their very sound says what he means. He is urging Mr. Lawrence, whose labors presumably are as arduous and exhausting as his own, to rest with him and relax from the cares that beset them both. Now that it is winter, he says, cannot we simply sit by the fire on certain days and waste our time gracefully? The winter then may seem less long than it does now; soon spring will have come again, reawakening breath in the ground and restoring color to those flowers Christ praised for never working at all, since they knew they would be taken care of by their maker. So it may be with us. What shall we eat and drink, and what music shall we hear, played on the gentle lute or sung to some excellent Italian air? It is wise to do this once in a while, my friend; as often at any rate as is necessary for the welfare of our souls.

Milton is saying this, and his sonnet is saying it with him. The first line, for example, begins with no such rush as we heard in the opening line of the other sonnet, where indeed an avalanche was starting on its way. "Lawrence, of virtuous father virtuous son"—the very gait of the syllables is gentle, as if the speaker bowed while he complimented son and sire. The rhyme sounds are tenor throughout; or else they are light and choice to suit the taste of connoisseurs, as the neat repast, the wine, and the Tuscan song will be. "A sullen day"—the phrase already conquers the weather it creates, making it seem a good thing to have outdoors, not indoors where the friends will sit. The movement of the poem is luxurious and relaxed, from phrase to phrase, from section to section; the octave and the sestet are properly separate, and within each of them the thought is developed with just enough complexity to tease the intellect of the listener but not with so much as to tax it. "What may be won from the hard season gaining"—perhaps we have to read this clause again in order to discover that it means "becoming gainers by as much as we may win from the season that in its hardness wins most of the encounters between us." The lily and rose are not identified, because for Mr. Lawrence, as for Milton, no reminder is needed of the Gospel according to St. Matthew. But the sestet is the triumph of the poem. "What neat repast shall feast us"—only the teeth and lips are required for pronouncing that, as only the teeth and lips will taste and sip the delicacies of this day. "Of Attic taste"—there it is again, "with wine": all light and choice, and fragile as the air these gentlemen will grace by breathing it. As music is

mentioned the sound of the words grows deeper and richer—
"hear the lute," and "warble immortal notes"—yet it will not
grow hoarse; nothing in this poem will ever disturb the clear,
smiling calm, the knowing and cultivated courtesy that Milton
has imagined for its medium. Such a medium provides the quiet
required by the last remark, with its understatement that only
Lawrence perhaps can be trusted to interpret rightly. "Is not
unwise"—the poem dies away on this accentless phrase, its content meanwhile having been absorbed by him who listens with
an answering smile.

The two sonnets are alike and different, as Shakespeare's
were. All four are successful beyond the dreams of most poets,
and yet no two of them could be mistaken for each other. It
was possible in Shakespeare's case to say that he did more in
one than he did in the other, and therefore that the one was
greater. In Milton's case comparison of any sort seems out of
the question, since there is nothing but a formal rivalry between the sonnet on a massacre and the sonnet suggesting din-
ner. Formally the two are equal. Which has the greater subject,
who will decide? Shakespeare had the same subject, love, in
both his poems, and in so far submitted himself to rule and
measure. Milton has two subjects, work and rest. Or wrath and
peace. Perhaps no man can judge the distance between them.

29. Sir Patrick Spens

The king sits in Dumferling toune,
    Drinking the blude-reid wine:
"O whar will I get guid sailor,
    To sail this schip of mine?"

Up and spak an eldern knicht,   5
    Sat at the kings richt kne:
"Sir Patrick Spens is the best sailor,
    That sails upon the se."

The king has written a braid letter,
   And signed it wi his hand,   10
And sent it to Sir Patrick Spens,
   Was walking on the sand.

The first line that Sir Patrick red,
   A loud lauch lauchèd he;
The next line that Sir Patrick red,   15
   The teir blinded his ee.

"O wha is this has don this deid,
   This ill deid don to me,
To send me out this time o' the yeir,
   To sail upon the se!   20

"Mak hast, mak hast, my mirry men all,
   Our guid schip sails the morne:"
"O say na sae, my master deir,
   For I feir a deadlie storme.

"Late, late yestreen I saw the new moone,   25
   Wi the auld moone in hir arme,
And I feir, I feir, my deir master,
   That we will cum to harme."

O our Scots nobles wer richt laith
   To weet their cork-heild schoone;   30
Bot lang owre a' the play wer playd,
   Thair hats they swam aboone.

O lang, lang may their ladies sit,
   Wi thair fans into their hand,
Or eir they se Sir Patrick Spens   35
   Cum sailing to the land.

O lang, lang may the ladies stand,
   Wi thair gold kems in their hair,
Waiting for thar ain deir lords,
   For they'll se thame na mair.   40

Haf owre, haf owre to Aberdour,
  It's fiftie fadom deip,
And thair lies guid Sir Patrick Spens,
  Wi the Scots lords at his feit.
                                    —ANONYMOUS

Some versions of this old Scottish ballad are longer than
we have it here, and many of them differ in other respects. A
popular ballad has no author as we know the term; it may have
had one once, but time and repetition have obscured his identity and altered his text—altered it in most cases by shortening
it until it contains only the essentials of the tale it originally
told. It was a song to be sung, and singers have an immemorial
tendency to forget, to improvise, and to improve. The great
virtue of any ballad is brevity—assuming, of course, a subject
with enough drama in it to invite intensification by abridge-
ment and omission.

The history of the present ballad is not our business here,
though it is well to remember that longer versions of it speak
of a voyage to Norway to bring back the king's daughter; of
Sir Patrick's safe arrival there; of a quarrel between his nobles
and the nobles of Norway, who accuse the Scots of staying
too long and wasting their host's food and drink; of Sir
Patrick's resolution to sail for Scotland even though he is ad-
vised that the sea is unsafe; of his sailing nevertheless; and of
the wreck with which every version ends. The shipwreck was
the heart of the ballad, as calamity is likely to be the stuff of
any popular narrative.

The present version is the classic one, and serves best to
show how a ballad should be constructed, and why it is so
difficult for a single author in sophisticated times to capture
the secret of the art. Line 41 is the only residue of the return
voyage; otherwise we should suppose that the ship was
wrecked soon after it first set sail, and indeed most readers do
naturally suppose this. We shall suppose it too, and forget

everything except the lines before us. They constitute a masterpiece of the ballad art, which is both a lyric and a narrative art since its aim is to sing—briefly, without taking breath—a human action, and to make it as moving as the sweetest song can be.

This song of Sir Patrick Spens is a series of lyric scenes with every transitional or explanatory passage left out. All we are told is that the king asks for a sailor; that an elder knight recommends Sir Patrick; that the king sends him an order and he receives it; that he laughs at first, then weeps at the thought of certain death, and wonders who has brought it on him; that nevertheless he rouses his crew, saying they will sail tomorrow; that one of them protests, foreseeing a storm; that they sail as scheduled; that the ship sinks, leaving only their hats on top of the water; and that their ladies will wait a long time for their return, seeing that they lie fifty fathoms deep, halfway between somewhere and Aberdour. We are told, certainly, a great deal in eleven ballad stanzas; but that is the point. There could have been many more stanzas, and much more detail. As it is there seems to be nothing that we could do without; and everything we are given is musical and moving. Not merely is no mention made of the king's starting to talk as he drinks his blood-red wine, or of his decision to write a letter, or of Sir Patrick's resolution to overlook the danger he faces, or of who it is that has seen the old moon in the new moon's arms, or of the storm itself and the sinking of the ship. A hundred other items are equally ignored—everything, indeed, except that essence which cannot be ignored if the poem is to exist at all.

The genius responsible for our song wastes no time on things we cannot instantly and deeply feel. It is not the facts that matter, or the reasons for the facts; it is the feeling—the pity of it, seeing how well these men were aware that they would die. Twice only does the ballad develop anything at length, and both times it is something to that point: first, the premonition of the men, and last the sorrow of their wives. Out of the forty-four lines as many as sixteen (15-30) are devoted to the one and as many as twelve (33-44) to the other. More than half of the poem, that is to say, concentrates upon the tragedy; less than half provides us with its framework. We have the minimum of deed and the maximum of desolation.

The poet is thus left free to do with his words what words in narrative song can best do—namely, enchant us. The bluff king, the quiet and perhaps cunning old knight, and the courageous crew whose members speak their minds so clearly, create a heroic setting which magnifies the disaster, but it is the disaster that moves us as only things both terrible and beautiful are able to move men. All is beautiful here, but we may not be sure of this until the last three stanzas, whose rhythmical, sweet movement, suggestive of a gentle sea that will bring the king's ship smoothly in, helps also to create the ladies with their fans and their gold combs who wait prettily for what the fair wind and the bright waves have in store. We know, of course, that they will wait forever; and so they seem to be doing as the poem closes. The repetitions in lines 33, 37, and 41 have done their work; they have raised the music of this narrative poem to the lyric level where all poetry, as poetry, is felt. The narrative was necessary, and indeed if it had not been perfect we should not be feeling what we feel in "fiftie fadom deip."

The art of poetry is the art of narrative too; no great lyric but tells its story, regardless of how much action was left out; no poem studied in these pages but somewhere—often in a middle stanza—reveals its concern with humanity in motion. But the final success, as even Homer knew, is when the story sings. That of Sir Patrick Spens sings in the memory of every person who knows it, and sings in the words of the poem itself. This is why there is no greater ballad, and possibly—for its length—no greater poem.

30. The Ballad of Father Gilligan

The old priest Peter Gilligan
Was weary night and day;
For half his flock were in their beds,
Or under green sods lay.

Once, while he nodded on a chair,   5
At the moth-hour of eve,
Another poor man sent for him,
And he began to grieve.

"I have no rest, nor joy, nor peace,
For people die and die";   10
And after cried he, "God forgive!
My body spake, not I!"

He knelt, and leaning on the chair
He prayed and fell asleep;
And the moth-hour went from the fields,   15
And stars began to peep.

They slowly into millions grew,
And leaves shook in the wind;
And God covered the world with shade,
And whispered to mankind.   20

Upon the time of sparrow-chirp
When moths came once more,
The old priest Peter Gilligan
Stood upright on the floor.

"Mavrone, mavrone! the man has died   25
While I slept on the chair";
He roused his horse out of its sleep,
And rode with little care.

He rode now as he never rode,
By rocky lane and fen;   30
The sick man's wife opened the door:
"Father! you come again!"

"And is the poor man dead?" he cried.
"He died an hour ago."
The old priest Peter Gilligan   35
In grief swayed to and fro.

"When you were gone, he turned and died
As merry as a bird."
The old priest Peter Gilligan
He knelt him at that word.   40

"He Who hath made the night of stars
For souls who tire and bleed,
Sent one of His great angels down
To help me in my need.

"He Who is wrapped in purple robes,   45
With planets in His care,
Had pity on the least of things
Asleep upon a chair."
—WILLIAM BUTLER YEATS

It is as rare as it is difficult for a successful ballad to be
written without the help of nameless collaborators after and
before. If Yeats has succeeded in this tale of an old Irish priest
whom one of God's archangels impersonated so that a dying
parishioner might not fail to be comforted, it is of course true
that he had one kind of collaboration which every intelligible
poet has. He could lean on institutions his society had made:
on Ireland, on its Church, on the tradition of the selfless old
priest whom his charges cannot live or die without, and on
the great legend of three supreme angels, Michael, Raphael,
and Gabriel, any one of whom may be sent by God to do

some good thing among men. Raphael, as companion and counselor of Tobias in the Apocryphal book of *Tobit*, represents the legend in its finest form. We see Raphael in that book, and we do not see his counterpart in this ballad—we only hear that Father Gilligan believes he came—but the line of descent is clear, and Yeats did not have to establish it.

Yet he had to write a successful ballad, and he did so—counting on others and then upon himself. His story is milder than the story of Sir Patrick Spens. The only death is that of a poor old man who in his last moment is merry as a bird. And the surrounding scenery, compared with Sir Patrick's stormy ocean, is domestic and familiar: evening moths, country fields, peeping stars, leaves in the wind, whispers in the dusk, and sparrows that chirp at the proper time. But Yeats needed as much art as Sir Patrick's unknown poet did, and he used as much.

His brevity appears in the lack of any transition between Father Gilligan's complaint (lines 9-10) and his cry of contrition (lines 11-12). The only connecting words are "And after"; we are expected to understand, and surely we do understand, that it is only because of his exhaustion during a time of plague or famine when half the people are sick and half are dead (lines 3-4) that his very bones have cried out, independently of him. "My body spake, not I!" In the same way we are led to infer that his fatigue continues even as he prays for forgiveness because he had complained (lines 13-14); not only continues, but lasts a long time—and here (lines 15-24) the poem itself grows long, and wanders among details. But as soon as the priest is awake the poem becomes as brisk as he; the horse is saddled and ridden off in no time at all, and only two lines (30-31) bring us to the sick man's door, which at once is opened by his wife. We are not told that Father Gilligan arrives; we simply see the door opening and hear the woman exclaiming: "Father! you come again!" The last word almost reveals the secret to us, but not to the priest who learns two lines later that the man is dead. His only thought is of the blessing he had failed to bring in time, and he sways in grief which is also guilt. Meanwhile the woman goes on to remark, as if she did not know what else was called for:

> "When you were gone, he turned and died
> As merry as a bird."

"When you were gone." Then he was here. Or someone was. But Yeats says nothing of all that; he simply has the old priest kneel and begin his second prayer. For Peter Gilligan understands what we understand, not only that he had been forgiven his outcry but that the cause of it had been seen by God Himself, Who then sent one of His great angels down to take his place till he was rested. The poor man had his blessing after all; and the old priest has had his miracle.

The art of telling a story is the art of knowing when to be short and when to be long. Yeats is aware of both necessities, and in two portions of his poem, like the author of "Sir Patrick Spens," he writes amply, as if time were no object. In lines 15 to 24 he halts his progress to assemble the soft things of the world that symbolize God's gentle intervention; and in the two final stanzas he stops altogether, leaving his hero lost in contemplation of the wonder that has occurred. The greatest being has known of the smallest; the maker of stars and planets, and the captain of the angels, has pitied the least of his creatures, an old priest asleep upon a chair. There is nothing about Father Gilligan's return home; nothing about what the woman does or does not understand; nothing about how or why Father Gilligan understood. There is only this hymn, this lyric conclusion, with its rapturous repetition of "He Who" and its innocent enumeration of God's grandeurs, to prove that Father Gilligan did understand. Of such for him was the kingdom of heaven. Of such for us is the kingdom of poetry.

GLOSSARY OF TERMS
Chiefly Metrical

Accent. Emphasis, beat, stress. Specifically, its presence in any unit of an utterance, or any syllable of a line.

Alexandrine. An iambic hexameter line.

Alliteration. The repetition of a sound at the beginning of two or more words or syllables.

Anapest. A foot of three syllables, accented on the third.

Assonance. Imperfect rhyme, with identity between the vowel sounds but not the consonants.

Ballad. A simple, short narrative in verse, adaptable to the singing voice.

Ballad stanza. A quatrain conventional in ballads and similar poems. Normally the first and third lines are iambic tetrameter, unrhymed, and the second and fourth lines are iambic trimeter, rhymed.

Blank verse. Unrhymed verse. Used almost invariably of unrhymed iambic pentameter verse.

Caesura. A break or pause, determined either by the sense or by the rhythm, within a line. Usually near the middle, but not necessarily there.

Consonance. Imperfect rhyme, with identity between the consonants but not the vowel sounds.

Couplet. Two lines in succession, rhymed.

Dactyl. A foot of three syllables, accented on the first.

Dissonance. Imperfect rhyme; *consonance* in its harshest form.

End-stopped line. A line whose rhythmical conclusion coincides with the conclusion of its sense, or with a natural pause which it indicates to the reader.

Feminine ending. In iambic verse, a final foot followed by an unaccented syllable.

Feminine rhyme. Agreement of sound between both syllables of two or more feminine endings.

Foot. A metrical unit, consisting of two or more syllables accented as the metrical pattern prescribes.

Free verse. Verse without metrical pattern.

Heptameter. A line with seven feet.

Heroic couplet. A couplet in iambic pentameter.

Hexameter. A line with six feet.

Iamb. A foot of two syllables, accented on the second. *Iambic.* Pertaining to this.

Iambic pentameter. A line with five iambic feet.

Italian sonnet. (Also called *Petrarchan sonnet.*) A sonnet in two parts. The first part, or *octave*, consists of two quatrains identically rhymed (abbaabba). The second part, or *sestet*, consists of six lines ending in new rhyme sounds, arranged in any of the several possible patterns (cdecde, cdeecd, etc.).

Masculine ending. In iambic verse, a normal final foot.

Meter. Measure. In poetry, the arrangement of rhythm in a system or pattern. *Metrical.* Pertaining to this.

Octave. See *Italian sonnet.*

Ode. A lyric poem, usually but not necessarily elaborate in its metrical pattern, and tending toward irregularity.

Onomatopoeia. The presence in one or more words of sounds or rhythms suggestive of the sense.

Pentameter. A line with five feet.

Quatrain. A series of four lines, rhymed abab, abba, or possibly otherwise. May stand alone, or may serve in a poem as a stanza or other verse unit.

Refrain. The more or less regular recurrence in a poem of a phrase or line with little or no modification, often at the ends of stanzas.

Rhyme. Identity in the terminal sounds, both vowel and consonant, of two or more words, considered either by themselves or as terminal words of lines.

Rhyme scheme. A pattern of rhyming in a series of lines, a stanza, or a whole poem.

Run-on line. A line, normally with no punctuation at the end, whose rhythmical conclusion does not coincide with the conclusion of its sense, which is postponed to the next or any later line.

Scansion. The process of scanning or analyzing the metrical structure of a line or series of lines.

Sestet. See *Italian sonnet.*

Shakespearean sonnet. A sonnet consisting of three quatrains, alternately rhymed, and a concluding couplet (ababcdcdef-efgg).

Sonnet. A poem of fourteen iambic pentameter lines, rhymed in pattern (See *Italian sonnet* and *Shakespearean sonnet.*)

Spondee. A foot of two syllables, both accented.

Stanza. A series of lines, fixed in the pattern of its meter and rhyme, and forming a regular unit in a poem of which it is a part.

Stress. See *Accent.*

Syllable. The minimum and basic metrical unit. A word, or a part of a word, producing in pronunciation a single sound.

Syntax. Sentence structure; pattern of meaning or sense.

Tetrameter. A line with four feet.

Trimeter. A line with three feet.

Triplet. Three lines in succession, usually of uniform length and rhymed, though the third line may be longer or shorter than the other two, and the rhymes may be involved in a larger pattern.

Trochee. A foot of two syllables, accented on the first. *Trochaic.* Pertaining to this.